All you need to know about

Leadership

and

the Eleven Roles of the Leader

A primer for managers and aspiring managers, and for top guns
in small teams and work groups

George Krasker

authorHOUSE®

AuthorHouse™ UK Ltd.
500 Avebury Boulevard
Central Milton Keynes, MK9 2BE
www.authorhouse.co.uk
Phone: 08001974150

First published by AuthorHouse 12/17/2008

ISBN: 978-1-4389-0053-7 (sc)

Printed in the United States of America
Bloomington, Indiana

This book is printed on acid-free paper.

krasker@gmail.com

Leadership is taking people where they haven't been before *(Anon, quoted by Andy Roxburgh)*

Leadership is the ability to win the hearts and minds of people in the achievement of a common purpose.

(The Leadership Trust)

Table of Contents

A Cautionary Tale

In the fight to keep his store from going under, Chris decided to change the way his staff worked. "Joe, from now on you'll take responsibility for purchasing. Make sure you know every supplier, and get to know some more firms so that we can buy where the value's best." "But Chris, I've only just started serving at the counter. I was just getting the hang of the job." "Sorry, Joe, you'll have to learn a different approach – and, by the way, your hours will change, so that you can be here early to check the lorries and their loads when they arrive." "But Chris..." "That's enough, Joe. Now, Lucy, you'll go on the counter in place of Joe. That'll mean leaving whatever you're doing in Accounts and learning to smile at our customers." "Chris, does that mean that I'll have to dress smartly and wear make up?" "Yes, Lucy – but don't expect an allowance in your pay packet for the extras." "Oh, Chris, you know I'm saving up to get married." "Sorry, Lucy, that's the way it is."

And so it went on. Nearly everyone in Chris's store had a new job, starting tomorrow. And Chris wasn't going to stand for any argument. He had made his decision, and that was that. The store was on its way to beating the only competitor in the town and becoming a monopoly, able to name its own prices, with obvious benefits to Chris, who was the owner as well as manager. That was how he had planned it (though he kept his plan to himself, in case his staff talked and the competition got to hear about it).

Within a few weeks, the staff had got to grips with their new jobs, but no one was happy. Some of them felt that a little training would have helped. And quite a few thought that they were doing a job that was beneath them – and a few more found that they couldn't cope with the complications of the new job – and they couldn't ask Chris, because his answer was always, "Just give it a few more days, and you'll soon get the hang of it." Chris also made sure that none of them could discuss their problems with the others, because he had ("for reasons of efficiency") got rid of the coffee machine and told everyone to bring their own tea or coffee and to drink it at their workplace.

Chris was happy with his handiwork. The store did well – Chris was sure that his changes had made the difference – but he hadn't noticed that everyone else in the town was doing well too. Everyone but Chris realised that their increasing turnover could be attributed to the car plant's prosperity, with its increased overtime and higher wages. Chris felt that he didn't need to pay higher wages in the store – "They earn enough as it is" – but he did close the store at noon on Saturdays instead of 4 pm. "Why should I pay them more for a shorter week?" And it meant that he could watch Hamford United without feeling guilty about leaving the store to run itself.

But increasing business meant more work for Chris. VAT and accounting, stock control, new stock layout to meet changing customer demand, new regulations and by-laws (the council was keen on adopting the latest EU legislation) and occasional problems of supply (Joe's suppliers had a habit of withholding deliveries until they were paid) – added to all this were his problems at home, his team wasn't doing well in the league and his ten-year-old car wasn't running too well, either. So he started to sleep badly, became bad-tempered, and who suffered? The staff, of course. Lucy and Joe sulked and were rude to their customers and suppliers, while most of the others slipped out to the back from time to time to enjoy a cigarette and a chat while Chris coped with his problems in the office.

Occasionally Chris thought he ought to ask one of the more mature people in the store to help with his backlog of work, but then he thought, "Who could I ask? I can't trust any of them to do a job the way I want it done, and anyway there isn't one who would actually want to run up the accounts, or deal with the taxman, or find a better way to handle stock control. I can't even ask one of them to take the money to the bank every evening."

Joe left to work at the factory, and earn better money. Chris asked the employment agency to find a replacement – and it turned up trumps; a graduate, looking for a six-month stint in retail during his gap year, applied, and Chris was delighted to take him on. James was keen, and knew a thing or two (his Dad gave him advice) – he asked for, and got, a better wage than Joe's and Chris agreed that he could go on a three-day course to learn a little about customer service. After a month, Chris's customers noticed a different attitude at the counter, and some of them told Chris that he had "hired a real good 'un." Chris was delighted.

One day, James walked into Chris's office (without knocking!) and hesitantly suggested that he could change the way the stock control system worked – using a computer instead of pen and paper. At first Chris was sceptical, but then he thought it was worth a try. "But in your own time, lad, not in mine." So James stayed late in the store some evenings, and pretty soon showed Chris the results. The first time *round, James had got some things wrong. Chris questioned some of James's assumptions – "We can't expect next-day deliveries from that Scottish supplier. And most of those items come from China, so we have to buy in larger quantities to cope with longer lead times, and that means more shelf space." So James worked on his ideas for a couple more weeks, and came up with a system that looked really good, a vast improvement on the old pencil-and-paper system. Chris had to invest in a new computer program, of course, but after a month, the results were looking very good.*

Chris began feeling better (a new car and an improved football team, now sponsored by the car factory, helped a lot). But James was now bored; he had done a good job on stock control, but serving behind the counter wasn't his idea of fun. Besides, he had another three months to run in Chris's store. Chris saw James's lacklustre attitude and wondered if he dared ask James to do another "little job" for him. "James, I wonder if you could give me a hand with the VAT returns?" Delighted, James sat himself down in the office after the store closed, and within two weeks had brought the books up to date – just in time for the visit by the VAT man, the first time that the returns hadn't been sent back for amendment. Chris gradually came to realise that he hadn't been doing too well on his own, and that inviting help for some jobs was key to keeping his own head above water, let alone the store's.

Then a new by-law meant that all employees had to wear special clothing, according to the jobs they did. Chris wondered how he could deal with this; each employee had to have a hat, coat, gloves and shoes specially designed for the job. And this meant a huge outlay, on two sets of everything for each person, plus lockers for personal belongings, weekly laundry, replacements every six months or so... Where would he find the money? The problem worried him so much that, with the deadline fast approaching, he decided to share the worry with James. James thought just a moment, and then suggested that Chris ask all the staff for their ideas. "Can't do that!" said Chris, "They're too busy, and anyway they won't have any ideas that'll help us." "Try it," said James.

So Chris called the staff together (in their lunch-hour, of course – old habits die hard) and put the problem to them. "We all have to wear special clothes from Monday week," he said. "How can we find them and buy them before then?" "Just a minute," said James, who took a few minutes of everyone's time to explain what the new clothing was for, why it had to be worn and by whom, and the need for lockers. He then added, "Take a few minutes together over your sandwiches, and come back just before two to let us have your ideas." Chris was horrified; he'd never heard his staff being treated like that.

At five to two, the whole group met again. The staff had elected a spokesman, Bill, who slowly and carefully explained how the group had thought about it and, although they weren't happy with the new rules, they saw that they had to comply. "So Daisy called the local laundry, and they said that we can hire everything that we need, and it all includes laundry and replacement. And Jim and me, we'll make some lockers out of the crates that come from China, and we'll set them up in the little room next to the store-room, where you have the safe. We can't say better than that."

Chris couldn't believe his ears. The problem had gone away!

And the store prospered, and the staff were happy (especially when Chris was elected to the local council, which made him a hero) and James decided to delay his gap-year plans by six months and help with setting up training and development programmes for everyone (including Chris), and soon people were coming to the store to ask if perhaps there was a job vacancy? And Chris, still the manager but glorying in his new complementary role as leader, got the staff together occasionally to talk about the future, and invite discussion, and hear about issues that seemed to be important.

And a big multinational chain wanted to buy the store, and Chris and the staff (including James) said, "No."

All you need to know about
Leadership

Leadership is like air: necessary for life but impossible to see or touch.
(Japanese saying)

Introduction

The early-retired managing director of a British engineering firm told me, "A manager is deemed to be a leader." We argued, my position being that this "deeming" does not make it so, and that many managers have not used or developed the leadership traits that are inherent in them. I have also found that those who do the "deeming" are confused between *management* and *leadership*. My friend defended his point of view, claiming that leadership is in the minds of those who follow, those who report to the manager. I couldn't disagree with this, but felt that there must be a distinction between leadership as perceived and management as enacted. This book is the result.

Leaders have been a part of the human race since time began. Their characteristics as leaders have been developed over many generations, which is why much of the content of this book consists of 'eternal truths' and homilies, of which we need to be reminded from time to time. There's nothing new in here – simply my compendious summary and interpretation of what has been said and written about leadership in the last few years.

On the other hand, management was an innovative concept a mere century or so ago, when managers were a new breed invented by factory owners and businessmen, who saw a need for delegating authority to, and establishing channels of communication through, intermediaries between them and the ever-growing workforce. The business world is still coming to terms with the implications of employing managers to monitor and control its functions. *Do managers contribute to productivity, profit and growth? What are the criteria for their selection? How should they be developed and trained? How important is leadership in their attitude towards those who report to them? And in the ways in which they perform their duties?* Managerial skills are now recognised and taught, although management is still not recognised as a profession.

What does the Manager do?

The manager is a key figure in today's workplace, and he learns his transferable skills through training and experience. He passes them on to his successors. He practises his skills daily, throughout his (managerial) working life. His portfolio of competences is wide-ranging, demanding, and increasing all the time. Charles B. Handy paraphrases Mintzberg (*"The Nature of Management Work"*) in reporting that the manager's roles include "leading, administrating and fixing." Under 'administrating', the manager demonstrates his acquired skills of

- evaluating and forecasting
- planning and resourcing
- controlling and monitoring
- training and coaching.

'Fixing' involves
- dealing with crises and unpredicted events
- allocating resources
- negotiating
- entrepreneurship.

The role of 'leading' in a manager's portfolio is the additional human dimension, the interpersonal behaviour needed to help people to meet and exceed expectations in their contributions to the manager's 'administrating' and 'fixing' roles. It is this responsibility of leadership that we are dealing with in the book. (It includes the training and coaching listed under 'administrating').

And we're not talking only about managers in business and industry. Examples of managerial look-alikes are found in politics, in voluntary organisations, among parents and teachers, in team sports and in hundreds of other common situations in today's complex world. The term 'leader' is frequently misused for these people and their positions. In many cases, some or all of the eleven key leadership roles are not used, not required or are even contrary to the task in hand. For example, the negative view in the press of the 'leadership' of a former manager of England's national soccer team, Kevin Keegan, was unjustified; he should have been judged on his performance, not as leader, but as the manager of the team (and been found worthy).

Recent thinking on management organisation focuses on the notion that *"Leadership can exist anywhere in the organisation"* (The Industrial Society, "Liberalising Leadership"). Everyone has leadership potential which can be drawn out by opportunity, encouragement, example, correction – from other leaders, from mentors, even from the 'followership'. When the potential is realised, when leadership behaviour contributes to the group's performance, everyone benefits. The manager who demonstrates effective leadership behaviour in addition to his formal managerial skills is more productive than a manager whose leadership behaviour is flawed or absent. His subordinates are more likely to achieve their individual and collective goals.

> ...the maximisation of the human resources which, at its best, amounts
> to effective leadership. *("The Manager as Leader", The Industrial Society, Notes for Managers 14)*

Selection of managers in industry and business has become less focused on learned skills, on diplomas and certificates, and more on personal characteristics and experience. "Let's see what sort of person you are," say the selectors. The traits that are sought include the Eleven Roles of the Leader, described in the following chapters, with the implication that leadership behaviour, with its focus on human relationships, is valued as much as acquired skills. And latent leadership skills can be discovered, then developed and nurtured, for the benefit of the organisation.

The Concept of Leadership

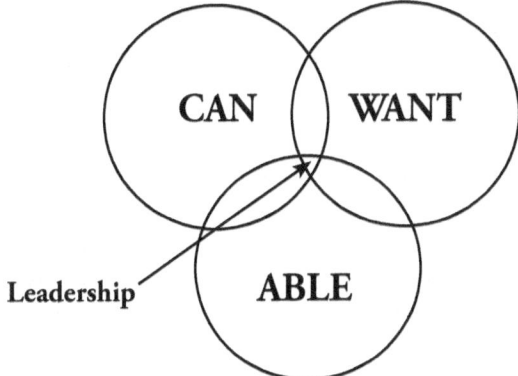

A three-circle diagram is often used to describe concepts such as 'work'. Here, we use it to identify the components of leadership. Each circle represents one aspect of leadership. "Can" represents the *permission* to lead, accorded by the situation (partly constant, partly changing), the followers and the larger organisation. In this book, we take this permission for granted, but acknowledge that a leader owes his claim to the leadership role, firstly to the followers, secondly to the situation and thirdly to those to whom he is accountable.

"Want" refers to the *desire and intention* to lead. You would not be reading this book if you did not have a mind to lead people (in addition to your managerial tasks). Like *permission*, your drive to adopt the Eleven Roles of the Leader, in order to become a more effective manager, is also taken for granted. (Throughout this book, "effective" describes the expending of effort in the right place, at the right time. The amount of effort is immaterial.)

It is the third circle that this book is about. "Able" means your proficiency to behave, in appropriate situations, as a leader. It means knowing when and how to apply leadership behaviour effectively. It implies awareness of the value of the Eleven Roles of the Leader in formulating and achieving the goals of the group of people to which you belong.

Why Managers?

Managers are a vital and indispensable part of the hierarchy of most successful business organisations. Most of them manage people. So do

- foremen
- supervisors
- team leaders
- shop stewards
- heads of department
- senior partners
- directors
- chief executives.

They are expected to manage people – factory workers, knowledge workers or simply members of the group – to produce results. They are essential for the proper continuous functioning of the organisation. But, as John Farrow wrote in 1991, *"Complex organisations staffed with motivated professionals need leaders first and managers second"*. It's like buying a car; you expect to get four wheels and other parts that make it work. It's the 200 horsepower and custom interior that attract you and raise the car, in your eyes, to something worth owning. In the same way, managers are expected to forecast, to plan, to command, to co-ordinate, and to control. But it's his leadership behaviour which raises a manager above the average, in the eyes of his followers, his peers and those he reports to.

Leadership comprises behaviours that are inherent, that can be practised, and that can be 'sharpened' to improve the performance of the individual and of the group to which he or she belongs. Leadership is not a skill to be taught and learned from scratch, tested, recognised by diploma, rewarded and passed on. On the contrary, being inherent, it can be encouraged and developed. Some individual behaviours can be taught and learned – for example, the 'rules' of delegation. But when change is required, when people are to be taken where they haven't been before, the manager-as-leader uses normal, natural, well-sharpened leadership behaviour to ensure a successful outcome.

Leadership traits such as trust, trustworthiness and delegation don't come easily and naturally in today's cynical and aggressive world. They are not normally encouraged in managers – but they are essential in leaders. We'll look at these traits, and identify ways in which they can be developed as a part of every manager's portfolio of skills.

A manager who does his prescribed job well is an asset to the business, but one who exercises leadership as well has value beyond his position. Managers can, of course, improve their performance by developing and sharpening those 'people' skills which are required of a manager: organising, controlling, appraising, coaching and the rest. A manager may embrace processes such as continuous improvement, organisational effectiveness and the quality-directed competences that have been introduced ever since Deming gave us Total Quality Management. But if his leadership potential is not fully developed or applied, his ineffectiveness as a leader spoils his achievements as a manager.

Experienced managers will say that this is all old hat, that there's nothing new in all this. Maybe so, but a reminder of these precepts for better managing can do no harm. If you are an experienced manager, take the time to revisit the rules and formulae relating to your professional skills, of showing that you are a self-developer (part of Role number 10) and that you can refresh your managerial performance for the good of the group you are part of. And if you are known for employing leadership behaviour successfully, you may still need a reminder of some of the little details that make the difference between sound leadership and highly effective leadership.

After reading this book you will be able to

- separate the *function* and *skills* of management from the *roles* and *behaviour* of leadership
- identify and describe the behaviours that constitute the continuing process of leadership, and thus analyse your behaviour as a leader
- determine in which leadership characteristics a shortfall can be rectified, and so achieve your leadership potential in order to improve your performance as manager, and the performance of your group. In this way, your latent

leadership behaviour can be developed and brought to bear on everyday managerial tasks and responsibilities.

By deconstructing the term 'leadership', this book offers ways to understand what it is and how it works. There are hints and tips to help you achieve success in behaving like a leader, especially *more* success if you are already a manager in charge of a group of people.

Not only managers

You don't have to be called a manager to be a leader. Effective leadership by anyone heading up a group of people can contribute to group effort. The chairman of the committee, the leader of the gang (the ringleader), the owner of the supermarket, the staff nurse and the captain of the netball team can all raise the performance of the group they are part of simply by behaving as leaders when the situation arises.

These are among the many people who bear the same responsibilities and share the same tasks as managers in industry and business. For example, unpaid officers in voluntary organisations are expected to organise, resource, monitor, control, train and produce results in the same way as salaried managers. Leadership behaviour is precisely the same for paid and unpaid managers. It is probably more demanding for the unpaid, since their followers (volunteers all) can absent themselves without leave – or simply walk away at any time and on any pretext! Some businesses recognise the exceptionally high value of leadership behaviour in voluntary organisations, and advise their managers to emulate the ways in which unpaid managers behave.

Leaders-to-be and newcomers to management can also find value in the following chapters. A leader may emerge from the ranks without warning, and in unplanned ways. A person may instinctively reveal himself or herself as a leader by asking during a meeting, 'Why are we here?' or 'What is the *real* problem?' To show that it's not just a matter of playing devil's advocate, he or she follows up on the question by proposing a positive way forward for the group. Or a future leader offers a problem-solving strategy that is beyond the current thinking of the group – a 'could-be' idea when others are thinking of 'should-be' – and then defines the path that takes the group to this new state.

Using this book, an aspiring leader can try out his or her delegation talents, or sharpen his or her communication proficiency, so that when the call comes, he or she has confidence in at least some aspects of his or her leadership behaviour.

The people who are led (the 'followers') can use this book to evaluate the leadership qualities of the people who lead them. They can assess their behaviour as leaders and, where 360-degree feedback is part of the performance appraisal process, give a manager something to think about and, if necessary, take action on.

'He' and 'she', quotations and teams

From this point in the book, I've stuck with the convention of 'he' and 'his' when referring to the leader, to followers, to delegates, and other people. I don't like the modern ungrammatical use of 'they' when referring to an individual. I've used 'he or she' in the previous paragraphs, and found that it's an obstacle to readability. ('He' appears over 500 times in the rest of this book!) I take for granted that women who read these words understand that I do not intend to ignore or slight them. On the contrary: **women leaders** are today demonstrating that they are as effective as men, provided that they are not handicapped by the 'glass ceiling' nor aggressively competitive with their male counterparts.

In fact, women exhibit characteristics that, in many situations, make them better leaders than men. These characteristics include diplomacy and tact, understanding and sympathy, openness and trust, which enable them to resolve conflict and maintain a stable working atmosphere more effectively than many men can. Women encourage participation, share information, instil group identity and know how to lead without formal authority. In addition, women are more subtle and more polite than men. They may sometimes not display the same drive and obsession with results as men do, but on the contrary women are more careful and cautious, and take fewer risks. Generally, women's focus on people rather than on the task makes for more productive intra-group relationships and for more emphasis on personal development and self-management.

Quotations: other people have expressed their thoughts on leadership and related subjects more succinctly than I can. Quoting them highlights the number and variety of people who have expressed their views. [I have added my own comments to some of the quotations, in square brackets.] The bibliography at the end of the book details many of the sources.

Leadership is not necessarily **team-building**. The 'team' word is not part of the vocabulary in this book (except in the clichés 'Virtual teams' and 'team spirit'), fashionable though it is. 'Team' means, to me, a group in which each individual's contribution is essential for success – without this contribution, the enterprise will probably fail. Examples of collaborative teams like this are found in soccer, in filmmaking, in a restaurant kitchen, among circus acrobats, in a submarine crew, on a car production line. But in most situations in business and voluntary organisations, although each individual contributes to the result, each contribution is not essential for success, and the absence of a player does not automatically mean failure.

As a way of describing a number of people who share a common objective, short-term or long-term, and among whom the absence of one member is a nuisance but not worse, I prefer 'work group' or **group** – the average work unit in today's workplace, or the average committee. It may be a department of one hundred people marketing a range of products, or a company employing thousands, or even a small, close-knit amateur drama group. Leadership behaviour is essential for the proper functioning of them all. Any of these groups should have a leader who can influence morale, create unity of effort and inspire achievement, thus creating the 'team spirit.'

Personality versus behaviour

By setting high standards and describing how to achieve them, this book can help the reader to become a better manager of people through leadership. And individual chapters may prove helpful to people without leadership aspiration. For example, "The Communicator" can be read by anyone who wants to improve his presentation skills, or who wants to run meetings more effectively.

What follows is a series of ways in which a person can change aspects of

- his behaviour
- his moral conduct
- his treatment of others

to enhance and exercise his inherent leadership potential, for the benefit of the group of which he is a member. And it has to be a gradual process: an old rule of thumb used by parents and teachers to help people to change their behaviour is that a bad habit cannot be changed at a stroke, but requires gradual coaxing to turn into a good habit.

But we cannot ask anyone to change his personality, nor should the following chapters be thus interpreted. Let's be clear about one thing. Personality can't be changed. I. L. Child's definition of personality helps us to understand this: '*Personality is more or less stable internal factors that make one person's behaviour consistent from one time to another, and different from the behaviour other people would manifest in comparable situations.*' Personality characteristics are inherent. They may change over time, to a small degree. They can be deliberately changed by the individual, but only with considerable effort and determination. They influence our behaviour, and they are perceived by others as the Real Us. Examples of personality traits include

- Naive/stern
- Wavering/industrious
- Warm/cold
- Rude/polite
- Cruel/humane
- Cautious/impulsive
- Strong/weak
- Innovative/adaptive
- Honest/dishonest

By contrast, leadership is a matter of behaviour, which can more easily be changed. This is the message of this book: **change your behaviour to become a better leader**. Examine your strengths, decide which leadership characteristics are strong within you, and exploit them. Then work on those other aspects of your behaviour which, in terms of leadership, can be improved. A flaw in only one leadership characteristic may result in poor or inadequate leadership, so effort put into developing your weak points until they reach the same effectiveness level as your strong ones will inevitably result in more effective leadership behaviour.

If you agree with the analysis of leadership and its breakdown into the Eleven Roles, which follow, you might like to ponder on these questions:

- Does every group of people get the leader it deserves?
- Could we individually play a more pro-active part in the selection of our managers-as-leaders?
- Should *we* elect our managers at the office?
- Could *we* decide who should be 'rich and famous'?
- Could *we* nominate who will stand for election to Parliament?
- And, most relevant of all in the present context, should *we* decide once and for all whom we will follow and respect as leaders?

We are all leaders at one time or another. *(Charles B. Handy)*

The Value of Leadership

In our time you must convince people that you are leading them the right way, and that there's something in it for them. I think that very few executives have understood this up to now. (Reinhard Mohn, former CEO of Bertelsmann, quoted in TIME)

The adoption of leadership behaviour as a means of helping people to work together can have a huge impact on the results of their efforts. Everyone benefits: the individuals in the group, the leader himself and, of course, the organisation under whose umbrella the group exists.

What are the rewards of leadership behaviour for the **organisation**? There are eight main reasons for the organisation to encourage and develop leaders:

1. Group cohesion, leading to fewer changes of personnel, reduced training cost, higher group performance.
2. Pride in the organisation, leading to increased job satisfaction.
3. Group self-esteem in the face of competition and challenge.
4. Reassurance (for the group) in times of self-doubt; elimination of uncertainty.
5. A prop for the weak and hesitant, and a restraint on the impetuous.
6. A direction for the anxious, and a guide for the lost.
7. The creativity of discontent, the constant challenge that results in continuous improvement.
8. Confidence on the part of management, watching the group's performance, in the leader's abilities to help the group achieve its goals.

Just let me make one thing clear — my messages, on the behaviours that make a leader effective, are the icing on the cake, the deft brush-strokes that turn a good picture into a masterpiece, the little extra that turns failure into success. Most people, whether salaried employees or voluntary workers, are highly motivated to do what is asked of them, even to exceed expectations, whether the boss is a manager or leader. But if the boss adopts leadership behaviour effectively and consistently (but not inflexibly), the results will be signally better for the organisation than if he just bosses.

Effective leadership brings benefits in some situations, some of the time. However, leadership behaviour used all the time brings benefit to the larger organisation all the time. It helps the group through the changes and crises experienced by the organisation, it helps to develop future managers, and it has a positive influence on all stakeholders – customers, employees, shareholders and suppliers.

Rewards for the Group and its Members

The benefits to the group of effective leadership behaviour are, I hope, evident throughout this book. The group as a whole develops greater cohesion and energy if its direction is well defined, if the road it takes is clear of obstacles, and if it is empowered to act within its capabilities and comfort, even if it is stretched. The group's productivity and ability to meet its goals are enhanced.

With an effective leader, who expresses pride in the group's achievements, individual group members are inspired to perform to their utmost to achieve personal and group goals. They contribute effectively, not only to group performance but also to the organisation's strategy and innovation. They demonstrate enthusiasm and esprit de corps in the face of competition and failure. They behave as future leaders.

Rewards for the Leader

The manager who recognises the value of leadership behaviour as a component of his management skills portfolio is a better manager:

- his dealing with people, a key function of management, is easier and more fruitful.
- his self-confidence is high; his personal contribution to the organisation's performance, and that of his group, is respected and appreciated.
- he knows that he is doing his best to reach the highest level of managerial competence and effectiveness.
- he can expect to be recognised and rewarded for the results of his leadership behaviour.
- he has greater confidence in his management of the group.
- he is provided with resources to deal with unforeseen events.
- he has the satisfaction of seeing a job well done, knowing that his own can always be done better.
- and, if he has that kind of ambition, he can see himself as an 'intrapreneur' or even an entrepreneur.

The manager who has thought about his leadership behaviour knows the Eleven Roles, and evaluates his performance against each of them. He invites 360-degree feedback too, to learn about others' impressions of his performance as leader (and as manager). His awareness of the value of leadership behaviour is such that his conscious efforts to improve his performance inevitably make him a better manager.

It's not easy being a leader. Effective leadership is a permanent, long-term pattern of attitude and behaviour. Some of the leadership behaviours listed in this book simply don't work if they are switched on and off. For example, you cannot mistrust a person for a short time, and afterwards try to trust him. Integrity and trustworthiness are permanent assets. You can't use challenging behaviour once, and think that you have earned your leadership credentials – people will quickly perceive one-off, unrepeated (unrepeatable) behaviours. All leadership behaviour has to be consistent and constant, and complementary to managerial duties.

And constant leadership is hard work. To be a full-time active manager-as-leader requires, initially at least, effort and dedication. It probably needs a significant change in behaviour. But, with time, leadership behaviour comes naturally and easily, and the leader brings benefits to himself, the group and the organisation.

> Complex organisations staffed with motivated professionals need leaders first and managers second. *(John P. Kotter)*

Leadership styles

Leadership styles, from authoritarian to democratic, demand flexibility to be effective. Style is demonstrated in decision-making and problem-solving.

Much has been written on the ways in which leaders demonstrate different styles of leading. Most writers describe two opposing styles, at extreme ends of the spectrum, with just a few shades in between. Let's look at their views.

On one hand, there is the authoritarian, autocratic or 'push' style (useful when the focus is on task). This style of leadership is often from behind, and is displayed by the sales manager in his office, and by the general in his battle HQ. In contrast, there is the democratic or 'pull' style (when the focus is on people). This style of leadership is from the centre, visible (like Henry V before Agincourt), a role model. And finally there is the conventional style of leadership, from the front, aloof, isolated and expected.

The difficulty in applying these and other style theories to the behaviour of individual leaders lies in the absence of any identification of the grounds for a leader's effectiveness or lack of it. Defining a leader's style means describing the general behaviour that is perceived at any one moment. But we will see that leadership behaviour is composed of the Eleven Roles, and these are not described in discussion of styles. The Eleven Roles, in any case, are usually interspersed with managerial activity, thus diluting the opportunities for defining an individual's leadership style.

What others have written

Charles Handy writes of the authoritarian and democratic styles, but calls them 'structuring' and 'supportive' in order to lessen the emotional stress of the more widely used words. Another writer gives us 'automatic' and 'creative' leadership, which between them share the whole range of leadership behaviour and characteristics. **F.E. Fiedler** writes of the 'contingency theory' – the task-oriented style and the relationship-oriented style. Then there is the 'best-fit approach' in which an individual leader emphasises an appropriate mix of the three ingredients of leadership – the Task, the Support

Staff (the Followers) and the Leader.

Kenneth Blanchard's research identified four leadership styles: telling, selling, participating and developing. Choice of style is determined by the maturity of the audience (the followership), that is, by each individual's ability and willingness to do the job.

Bernard M. Bass writes that leaders may be laissez-faire, transactional or transformational. Laissez-faire leaders risk conflict and confusion by ignoring problems, refraining from intervening, not following up and avoiding taking a stand. Transactional leaders practise management by exception and use financial and psychological rewards for performance. [This may discourage initiative as well as being perceived as a substitute for effective leadership.] Transformational leaders change people's expectations of themselves and inspire their followers to high performance.

If the would-be leader wants to develop his leadership behaviour on the basis of a specific style, he finds little practical guidance. For example, trust is rarely mentioned in discussion of style, yet it is key to the relationship of a leader with members of the group. Similarly, skill in communication is vital to the effectiveness of a leader, yet little space is devoted to this important subject in any text describing leadership styles.

The Assertive (Authoritarian) Approach

The authoritarian style of leadership is better called "assertive" or "positive" since the aim of a leader in such a situation is to ensure that the group follows the course that he is convinced is the right one, and he persuades the group of his conviction. The assertive style may prove to be undesirable, since it encourages people to put more energy into avoiding mistakes than taking initiatives. It can lead to political manoeuvring and sycophancy.

There are occasions when a leader may have no choice but to be a driver (assertive):

- when he has special knowledge (confidential information, or special skills or experience)
- when he has a broad view, an overall picture (the 'helicopter effect') which others don't have
- when he has to overcome the resistance of an entrenched organisation with

6

established attitudes
- when, with constancy of purpose, he can stick to a long-term view.

An assertive leader may demonstrate the helicopter effect – that ability to rise above the situation and see what the situation calls for – when the task is more important than the people. He maintains a psychological distance from his group. The danger is that this separation from the group may become the 'ivory tower effect', in which imperfect communication (in both directions) results in a less than fully committed group. To avoid this, a leader should be capable of changing his style, from assertive (for long-distance vision) to co-operative (for sharing the perils of the journey). This is another instance where leadership complements and contributes to management behaviour, which is required to be flexible and change direction quickly.

Research by Fiedler, quoted by Handy, has been used to show that it is sometimes to the benefit of the group (and achievement of the task) if the leader is distant and task-centred rather than democratic. But Handy points out that Fiedler's research sample was flawed: it was small and untypical. However, the argument is still valid; there are times when an assertive, helicopter-effect leader has adopted the right style to lead the group effectively to success in its task.

> It is hard to look up to a leader who has his ear to the ground. *(James H. Boren)*

The Co-operative (Democratic) Approach

This style of leadership has the advantage of involving, at the 'vision' stage or at the planning stage, everyone who might be involved in the agreed action plan. It releases the energy and brainpower of the group, and allows its members to explore every avenue to success. Co-operative methods give everyone the chance to commit to the plan, and to feel that they have helped to make the decisions which led to the agreed plan of action. They know *why* the plan is important. All this depends, of course, on the manager-as-leader sharing all the information he has – information is power and must not be withheld.

When adopting the co-operative style of leadership, the leader understands the individuals he works with – which ones need pushing, which ones can be left to get on with the job, which ones to thank, which ones to flatter and nurture. He adapts his style to the individual. The leader also understands the group as a unit – how its members work together when making decisions, how their individual skills and personalities interact to meet objectives and perform tasks. He turns his knowledge into skill in handling the group. He delegates accordingly, he communicates appropriately, and he offers opportunities for development openly.

The co-operative approach may have some undesirable results:

- when decision-making is shared, empowerment is at its extreme; the leader must be prepared to lose control
- an outcome that may reflect what's wanted rather than what's needed
- it may take more time and energy than the assertive approach
- participants in the process may be aggrieved if and when their contributions are rejected. This in turn weakens their commitment to the group's task or project.

Flexibility is the key

As a leader, you don't have to decide which style to adopt. Flexibility comes naturally. You automatically find yourself using the assertive style when the situation demands it:

- when you have information that the group doesn't have
- when the change you are describing takes the group towards a new, distant goal
- when you are confronting an insubordinate, self-willed or newly-formed group.

On the other hand, you adopt the co-operative style when you want to involve the group in making a decision, or in preparing an action plan. Group members learn to expect this flexibility. It doesn't faze them, nor does it affect the performance of the group. Rather the opposite: the leadership style adopted by you, the manager-as-leader, is always appropriate to the situation (as you see it) and group members will react positively to the firmness with which you demonstrate the style you have chosen for the moment.

Leadership in action

A leader may be born or made. The manager may be an imposed leader – a contradiction. Businesses as well as voluntary groups need leaders. Quality is a leadership issue.

> Leadership is giving support, explanations and interpreting information so employees can understand it. Leadership is developing consensus. Leadership is sometimes the ability to say 'Stop', to draw a line, to take the heat out of a conflict, to conclude a debate and get down to negotiations. Leadership is the courage to put a stake on an idea, and risk making mistakes. Leadership is being able to draw new boundaries, beyond the existing limits of ideas and activities. *(Pehr Gyllenhammar, former CEO of Volvo, quoted by John Adair.)*

How does Leadership manifest itself?

A group may acquire a leader in several ways. A leader may be appointed – that is, he may be appointed to a management position in which he seizes the opportunity to conduct himself as leader. Alternatively, a leader may emerge unexpectedly and in a situation where there is a leadership vacuum, or where leadership is not actively sought. Or a leader emerges when the group attaches value to the success of a task which requires co-ordination and communication.

In a time of stress and change, or when there is doubt and confusion, an aspiring leader may make his presence felt with a few thought-provoking words, or with a plan for action to overcome the problem. An aspiring leader may offer a vision (with a plan for achievement) even when there is no apparent need for change. A leader is often waiting in the wings for the opportunity to deliver his message. And the group will accept these aspiring leaders, even if only for the time being, to carry the banner, to take charge of the project in hand.

> (Leaders) step forward, to lead as needed, regardless of position. *(Daniel Goleman)*

In any newly formed voluntary or informal group, there is always one person who starts the process of organising or co-ordinating the activities of the group. It may be because of a louder voice, or a desire for efficiency, or a 'bossy' nature. Whatever the circumstances, this person initially takes charge – this is leadership of a sort. Later, leadership of the group may fall to a person better qualified

- by experience
- by earned or unearned respect
- by superior technical knowledge

and the group turns to follow this new leader. Later still, another new leader may emerge who can organise the group effectively to make progress towards a goal which he has envisioned and which he communicates (persuasively) to the group.

Sometimes a manager may be appointed to lead the group in the direction determined by corporate goals. Risk may be involved, and so may a lack of resources. Using his leadership skills, the manager-as-leader accepts the risks (and persuades the group to accept them), while the leader-as-manager deals with the lack of resources by re-assigning tasks or by commandeering additional resources.

Thus are some leaders made (by appointment) or born. The situations in which the earliest manifestation of leadership takes place are many and varied. It may happen in a meeting whose chairman or convenor unwisely dominates the discussion, or allows the meeting to drift, allowing an up-and-coming leader to seize the reins. It can happen in an office, a factory or a school staffroom, when one person voices (and guides) the views of a group at a time of change: thus are trade union leaders created. It can happen wherever people interact. It can happen when change is contemplated or forced upon the group: a leader appears, to bring order to the confusion and doubt.

Leadership is action, not position. *(Donald H. McGannon)*

As we know, leadership can come from any member of the group. It may come from someone who has not so far exhibited signs of leadership, or it may be demonstrated by a manager adopting his role as leader. In the workplace there is an advantage if it comes from the manager:

- he is a source of authority
- he has knowledge/information that others don't have
- his role as leader, in addition to his function as manager, reduces confusion inside and outside the group.

Forms of leadership

Various writers have described leadership as taking two forms, situational and forced (other terms used in place of 'situational' are *emergent* and *natural*). Situational leadership is that kind which manifests itself when the occasion arises. An example is the "informal" meeting, in which a discussion leader or an opinion leader may emerge. Another situation is the exercise in which a group of young cadets, aspiring to become army officers, have to cross an imaginary stream with a barrel, a rope and two poles. A leader always emerges from the group to direct the operation. Sometimes a second leader takes over, at a later stage of the exercise when the first leader has hit a problem.

> Leaders are needed at all levels [of the organisation] and in all situations.
> *(Charles B. Handy)*

On the other hand, forced or imposed leadership is a characteristic of many types of organisation. In being promoted to a managerial position, a man or woman is expected ("deemed") to take on a leadership role, without assessment of his or her capabilities as a leader. The new job will require specific management skills and traits which the incumbent possesses in plenty, but subsequent evaluation of the new manager's performance may include a judgement on leadership behaviours which were not listed in the job description, but which are vital to the successful execution of the job.

Most managers, in their new assignments, easily mitigate the problem of imposed leadership. They adopt their innate leadership behaviour and identify the opportunities to become successful leaders, almost by default, and even without knowing it. But there are others who, as imposed leaders, fail to realise the opportunity. The group is deprived of effective leadership until the new manager has, through experience and feedback, recognised and evolved his leadership potential.

Leadership in Business

The business world has need of leaders, and we can identify the challenges of leadership through the experience of managers and other employees at all levels of business. But the hierarchical and authoritarian nature of most workplaces discourages the adoption of some leadership behaviours such as trust, trustworthiness and delegation. This barrier to the effective application of leadership behaviour frustrates potential and aspiring leaders, but can give them energy and determination to exercise their talents and break out of the traditional managerial mould.

Where a manager is deficient in leadership behaviour, his subordinates tend either to be demotivated, without initiative and drive, or to act independently of the manager and his authority. As a group, they may conspire to bypass the manager, even to arrange his downfall. They may collectively agree to do no more than the minimum to execute the group's assignments. However, an effective leader can quickly and easily remedy this situation, and gain the co-operation and trust of his reports. He can take the group further, faster and deeper, with willing and participative people to do what is asked of them, by using appropriate leadership behaviour. (More about this in "Leadership and Management," page 99.)

> A leader is best when people barely know he exists, not so good when people obey and acclaim him, worst when they despise him. Fail to honour people, they will fail to honour you. But of a good leader, who talks little, when his work is done and his aim fulfilled, they will all say, "We did this ourselves". *(Lao Tzu, 604 BC)*

An experienced manager-as-leader adopts leadership behaviour routinely, without let-up. He assumes the leadership role even when dealing with people who are not members of the group. He uses his skills in challenging, communicating and envisioning and even delegates upwards to ensure that his bosses know what he is planning and risking, and how his group's performance is meeting the goals of the bigger organisation. He uses the same skills, especially his skills of persuasive communication, to influence his suppliers and his customers to advance towards the same visions and situations that he himself has planned.

> Leaders have to lead their bosses as well as their peers and subordinates – and other stakeholders too, such as suppliers and customers, *("Perspectives", IMD Lausanne).*

Leadership in Voluntary Organisations

In an attempt to help them handle their assignments more productively, several businesses in the USA and in Britain have invited their managers to look at the ways in which effective voluntary organisations work, and especially at the qualities that their leaders display. This is not surprising, since the characteristics of voluntary organisations demand the very highest degree of leadership behaviour. The leadership challenges of running a conventional shareholder-owned business are as nothing compared with managing, for example, a parent-teacher association or a sports club (the management skills, on the other hand, are much more important for the businessman).

It takes strong leadership to inspire volunteers to work towards a common goal, and to keep them motivated even though, as volunteers, they should know what they have let themselves in for. They can express their independence by walking away (together or in different directions) at any time. The leader needs to use highly developed skills of persuasive communication, praise and recognition of exceptional effort, and an inspiring vision to maintain the momentum of interest and energy. The leader needs to lead by example, to trust others, and to use good judgement to kindle respect, which is the substitute for the authority which is denied him.

When members of a club or society are connected by principle or belief, or when their affiliation to the group is of a fragile nature based on shared activity such as a sport, a hobby or community involvement, then leadership becomes a unifying factor, an essential for existence. The leader must weave a delicate path between assertiveness and cooperativeness to ensure that members of the group (which exists only for its members) feel as much involved in the running and development of the group as they want to be. The leader has little or no structural authority and no power to threaten or sanction. The ticklish and scrupulous leadership required in these conditions is an excellent model for salaried managers to follow.

Relevant skills (or sapiential authority) may also be needed by the leader in situations where skills are a key element in the activities of the group. The leader also needs to demonstrate trust and trustworthiness if the group exists to work with non-members as, for example, in aid and relief organisations. Some management skills are not appropriate, because authority is not assigned, external pressure to produce and perform is less onerous, and members are freer to express their views.

Leadership of a voluntary group may change either by popular decision, in which the group elects its own leaders, or through natural tendencies. The popular vote is a healthy phenomenon, since standing for election as leader displays commitment publicly, while electing a leader displays a group's confidence that is hard to deny later. On the other hand, where a leader is allowed to emerge naturally within a group assigned to a project or task, the leadership role may pass from one person to another, according to situation, in an apparently haphazard way. Lack of formality does not matter, however, as long as the group accepts each leader as such and allows him to fill the role effectively.

When studying the success of most voluntary organisations in acquiring effective leadership, the question arises: should we elect all of our leaders? The answer lies in our definition of a leader as a person who fills the *role* of leadership. He is not the person who is assigned, by others, to manage the group, using his managerial training, skills, power and authority in that *function*. A group of volunteers selects its own leader, by formal election or by natural acceptance of the person who takes the lead at one particular moment. In a strict sense, an imposed leader is a contradiction in terms; leadership cannot be imposed – it must be accepted.

Any situation can offer the opportunity for a wholly democratic selection of leader. Some voluntary organisations are a perfect example of a need for leadership fulfilled easily and effectively by purely democratic means. So are children's informal groupings, amateur sports teams and many affinity groups. In the working environment, a meeting or a short-term project provides an opportunity for the formal or informal selection of a leader, by the group or even by imposition from outside.

Judging the leader's performance

How does the leader know if he is successful? How can others judge a manager's performance *as a leader*? There is the task-effectiveness criterion; have the group's tasks been accomplished with the available resources? This is more a measure of managerial performance than of leadership. To judge leadership effectiveness, we look to the ways in which the manager has led the group, using all the leadership talents he possesses. And this is of paramount importance when appraising the performance of a manager: leadership is one of the key criteria for his success.

For a true picture of the leader, we study the attitudes and feelings of the group members. Does the group cohere, and work together as a unit? Are group members inspired, fulfilled, anxious for more of the same? Can they explain the leader's vision, his challenges, his methods of delegating and empowering? Can they give him high marks in each of the Eleven Roles? In short, do the followers believe that their leader is a good one?

We also invite 360-degree comment – from the leader's peers, from his superiors, from the people he interacts with outside the organisation. What are their comments on his conduct in each of the Eleven Roles?

The leader who passes this test can call himself a leader. He can write it into his CV. He can add the title to his business card. Until, that is, he is given the opportunity to earn his leadership credentials in a new group. He has to start again, and earn acceptance afresh, from peers, reports and bosses. It gets easier with each new assignment!

Beware of using style as a judgement factor. Research, quoted by Handy, shows that a supportive (co-operative) style of management leads to a more contented and more involved work group. Then he adds that style alone is not effective leadership. Style is a broad-brush view of a leader's performance. It doesn't allow evaluation or measurement, it doesn't include the detail of the Eleven Roles that we will describe, and it involves black or white judgements. For example, when a leader's style is described as either co-operative or assertive, there are no words or measurements to describe subtle variations between these two extremes. I repeat, leadership effectiveness can only be measured in the judgement of others.

The Quality question

Quality is defined as 'what the customer expects.' This is true in all situations, whether the 'customer' is an employee, a supervisor or a colleague or, outside the organisation, a purchaser, a shareholder or a supplier. In the leader's case, he has to interpret 'Quality' in terms of the people he has to deal with. He has to know what people expect of him and his group, and how to deliver it. What he thinks is right for himself may not appeal to others. He has to understand and interpret his customers' expectations.

The leader can only do his best. That is to say, he provides the kind of leadership that he thinks will meet the expectations of the followers and others, and meet the requirements of the situation. Here he takes note of two conflicting rules of Quality:

1. "The good is the enemy of the best", and

2. Churchill's "Do not let the better be the enemy of the good."

The leader balances these two equations, evaluating the risks versus the benefits. He compares the resources (time, cost, manpower, materials; available and deficient) against the desired outcome. He decides if the highest quality, with its high cost in resources, is really what the customer expects, or if the customer will be delighted if his expectations are exceeded (and will pay the price for it). Or maybe the customer will be satisfied with less, with a mediocre performance which can be achieved with fewer resources. He understands that perfection may not be desired or desirable. It's a tough decision. He may share it with the group.

If the leader, with or without the group, accepts the less resource-demanding solution, tolerance of mediocrity carries the danger that mediocrity is all there is, and a future demand for higher standards (of performance or result) will be ignored. Tolerance of this kind means setting goals that don't stretch the group. It involves giving fulsome praise where constructive criticism would be more valuable and appropriate. If, on the other hand, the leader opts for the solution which exceeds the customers' expectations, resource-hungry perfection may take time and energy which can be spent in more profitable ways.

The exact degree of quality required in any situation must be judged carefully and agreed by everyone concerned. There are times for expediency, where the goal has to be met within limited resources, and there are times when only the highest standard of output is acceptable. The effective leader has responsibility for this decision, though he takes account of the views of others.

The leader does his best. His best may be judged by others as exactly right for the situation or, alternatively, lacking in quality or too costly, and this will influence their judgement of his performance as leader. In the same way, he will use the 'Quality' issue to help him judge group members on their performance as followers.

Power and Authority

Power can be a useful tool, accompanied by responsibility. Abuse of power degrades the individual and the group. Three kinds of authority are linked to leadership.

Power is the ability to force people to obey, even reluctantly. Authority, on the other hand, allows orders to be voluntarily obeyed, in a 'comfort' situation. *(Max Weber)*

Power

Leaders may use power to establish and maintain their position. Not all the time, and not all leaders need this tool to strengthen their position – but in most instances, some kind of power is available in case of need. These are the options:

- physical power (used by muggers)
- legitimate power (used by the boss – also known as 'position' power or structural authority)
- referred power (delegated by the boss)
- resource power (used by finance directors and car-park attendants)
- expert power (derived from knowledge – also known as sapiential authority)
- information power (subset of expert power)
- negative power (the power to veto or deny access)

and any combination of the above.

The leader's use (or abuse) of any of these sources of power determines the degree to which the other members of the group accept his leadership. For example, in the first case (the mugger), acceptance is usually total, short-term, unrepeatable and very reluctant, because it is accompanied by the threat of violence. In the second and third cases (legitimate and referred power), acceptance is usually close to total, long-term and unquestioned.

Leadership is using your personal power to win the hearts and minds of your people to achieve a common purpose. *(The Leadership Trust)*

Power has its positive value. In group situations, power can be the driving force for

17

unity and consensus. Power can motivate (not only through threat of sanction), power can provide resources, and it can smooth a troubled path to success. Power can inspire respect and admiration, it can be envied and sought after and thus encourage personal development and progress. Power can make things happen.

On the other hand, abuse of power has become a matter of concern in many fields, from global politics and big-company affairs to amateur sport and education. Power gives people access to unmerited position, unearned wealth, or the opportunity to exercise sanctions over others. Many so-called leaders have used the power assigned to them, or seized by them, to adversely affect the lives of others, to enrich themselves, and to degrade the countries, businesses, and societies of which they are a part. In every case, they have chosen to ignore their responsibilities to the group, and have ignored all codes of ethical and moral conduct.

> All power is a trust. *(Benjamin Disraeli)*

The effective leader acknowledges and accepts the close connection between power and responsibility. He knows that his obligations include

- the burden of trust
- the loneliness of vision
- the fear of failure
- the threat of challenge
- the pain of change
- the insecurity of delegation
- the weight of integrity
- accepting others' perception that he is abusing his power.

None of these is unbearable, but their inevitability may come as a shock to a newly fledged leader. Leadership development may not prepare him for these responsibilities, and in defence he may adopt autocracy and 'bossiness' and abuse his power, with catastrophic results for both the leader and the group.

Authority

A leader has authority. It is a mix of moral, sapiential and charismatic authority.

- Moral authority is innate, born of experience. Moral authority comes from trust and trustworthiness, from clear-sightedness and tolerance, from consistency and integrity. It earns respect from the followers, who may prefer to feel that they work for the leader rather than for the larger organisation. Moral authority is essential for effective leadership.

- Sapiential authority, the skills and acquired knowledge possessed collectively by the group, is not essential in the leader. However, he needs to be clear about how much skill and knowledge he should possess in order to be effective. He may decide to acquire them through formal training and by working with group members. Alternatively, he may decide that group members can and should have more technical skill and knowledge than he has, in which case he never claims sapiential authority which he doesn't possess.

- Charismatic authority, that nebulous 'I know it when I see it' quality, is based solely on the perception of the followers and others. This perception can be heightened by the leader's impressive manner of communicating, his open door for help and counsel, his enthusiasm and determination, his evident self-confidence, and his trustworthiness. Followers, peers and bosses alike respect these characteristic behaviours, and group members in particular react positively to consistent displays of charismatic (as they see it) conduct. (See also 'Charisma' on page 131.)

The strongest foundation of the leader's position derives from his moral authority, which stems from his leadership behaviour. Perhaps the greatest leaders are those with no authority but the moral kind, and with no power with which to threaten their followers.

Sharpen your "Power and Authority" behaviour

- Know how to use the power available to you.
- Don't abuse it. Don't threaten.
- Accept the responsibility that power invokes.
- Decide how much sapiential authority you need.

Followership
and the transfer of leadership

*Followers **make** the leader, who inspires them, cares about them, and treats them as responsible and competent. Followers emulate the leader, respond to his lead and influence his behaviour through challenge and the threat of desertion. Unearned loyalty to the leader has little value. Changing his assignment lets a leader renew his 'followership' skills.*

Leadership is (also) about followership. You can only be the sort of leader that your followers are comfortable with. *(G Hofstede, "Culture's Consequences", quoted by Handy)*

Managers have subordinates, or reports, or associates. Leaders don't have subordinates; they have followers, colleagues, supporters, fans, disciples. These are the people who give the leader the opportunities to use his talents for a minute, a day or permanently. In most situations, these people (we'll call them followers) welcome the leadership that takes them where they haven't been before. In leaderless environments, the followers are lost and confused until a leader emerges. And when he does, followers become active group members in three distinct stages:

- First stage: a desire or need to be included – they bring conventional thinking to the group.
- Second stage: a demand for recognition – challenges are laid down as each new group member competes for his place.
- Third stage: a willingness to co-operate, to work with the other group members towards the group's goals.

From the outset, the leader treats his followers as competent and responsible individuals. He respects their capabilities, their aspirations and their needs, and sees his role as enabling and additive. He is sensitive to the expectations, values and skills of each individual with whom he interacts. He understands their moods, their weaknesses and their idiosyncrasies, individual by individual. He recognises that they need, even crave, discipline and guidance in the performance of their contributive tasks. He knows that leadership which is too strong and too overbearing may create dependency in the followers, a need to be cared for and told what to do, and an inability to take initiative. He must avoid creating comfort. He must inspire.

How does he know these things? Because he is, or has been, a follower himself, and realises that his position as a follower was exactly the reverse of his relationship with those who follow him now. He learns from the effectiveness and successes, mistakes and weaknesses of his own previous leader, and tries to emulate the one and avoid the other.

People frequently seek leadership, even expect it or demand it. "Tell me what to do" is frequently heard in any work situation, at home, or on the sports field. This is an opportunity for an aspiring leader, but it can also be a burden for the established leader. Delegation and empowerment offer relief from such day-to-day problems.

Leaders don't order or command, they inspire. *(Daniel Goleman)*

The leader shares the group's pains and pleasures, its setbacks and its successes, exploiting the energy thus created by both. Followers are inspired by the leader's example, not by his authority or power. At the same time, they take responsibility for challenging the leader's visions and decisions (if and when the leader makes autocratic decisions). Their trust in the leader is firm, yet they know as well as he does that he is fallible and that he welcomes constructive criticism.

The effective leader cares about the people in the group. He helps every group member to achieve his aspirations and to meet his goals. He inspires everyone to get the most satisfaction out of the effort put into achieving the group's tasks. He identifies and develops his successor. He watches the mood of the group and takes action if there are signs of distress or conflict. He supports and defends the group in its actions: his loyalty to the group is staunch and unyielding.

The leader respects individuals for what they are and can do, while helping individuals to improve their behaviour and skills. Followers, in their turn, accept that they are responsible for their own development. They take appropriate action to learn new skills and adopt new behaviours, and they share these aspirations with the leader. They treat him as a resource for personal development. They respect his opinions. Followers have to believe in the leader's understanding of their collective and individual situations, direction and motivation..

Example is another factor in the building of individual skills. The followers strive to emulate their leader's behaviour when they recognise its contribution to the common good. The leader encourages this. As a role model, he doesn't flinch at the mimicry he observes among the followers.

Communication within the group, often initiated by the leader and encouraged by him, builds trust and confidence. He uses "I" when asserting ownership of his visions and plans, and "we" whenever he talks about the group's goals and actions, and the reasons for them. Continuous and immediate feedback, by the leader, on the group's performance, and on the contribution of each individual, helps to build cohesion, efficiency and motivation, as well as developing skills and competence. Group members, in their turn, share their ideas, concerns and joys with the leader, always with the good of the group in mind, as well as their own personal wellbeing.

What others have written

Howard Gardner expounds the view that followers and leaders are bound by a common need for structure, hierarchy and a mission.

John Whitmore lists three stages in team (work group) development: followers first need to be included in the group, then assert themselves in seeking recognition, and finally co-operate when they know where they stand in the group. At the assertion stage, challenge may have to be met with an autocratic approach by the leader, who can also expect high levels of conflict and stress – and creativity.

Robert Kelley's ideas on followership include five types: sheep, yes-people, alienated followers, survivors and effective followers. They are differentiated by their passive or active followership, and by their thinking – independent, critical or dependent/non-critical.

The Leader as Member of the Group

An effective leader is part of the group – most of the time. On occasions, he will display the helicopter effect, rising above the situation to achieve a broad and distant bird's eye view of it. Or he may climb into an ivory tower, so that he can better think about the situation, analyse it and predict risk. But he cannot be an absentee leader, a remote-control leader, or a leader of more than one group at a time. He knows that he has to be perceived as a group member, wholly dedicated to the aims of the group – more dedicated, in fact, than the other individuals in the group.

> At his induction, the Bishop of Norwich was told by his predecessor, "Welcome to Norfolk. If you want to lead someone in this part of the world, find out where they are going. And walk in front of them." (*Jeremy Paxman, The English.*)

Followers respond positively to the leader's positive involvement in the group's tasks. This doesn't mean that the leader has to do everything that individual group members do, though it's an advantage if he has some of their skills and experience. In fact, it's possible that the leader is *less* qualified than others in the group. It is the leader's task, as it is the manager's, to encourage and allow 'subject-matter-experts' (SMEs) to use their expertise to the full, to help the group achieve its goals. The leader also knows that SMEs make their own contribution to the learning and knowledge of the group. Cross-fertilisation in a well-knit group can lead to unexpected and welcome results.

The size of the group is critical for effective leadership. If it is too big, the group becomes riddled with elitism and bureaucracy. It develops a gap between the 'top' and the 'bottom'. It loses its collective personality. Communication fails, and the group falls apart, often to be replaced with two or more smaller, more manageable groups. Not a bad thing, but best predicted and deliberately planned and executed. This is the time for a follower to become a leader, partly through encouragement, partly through the original leader's recognition of his potential.

The Obligations of the Followers

People have a right to effective leadership. But this right, like all others, brings obligations. Followers earn their leadership through dedication to the task(s) in hand, support for the leader's decisions (on those occasions when these decisions are assertive, made without consultation), and acceptance of the leader's weaknesses.

> A leader doesn't complain that his or her followers aren't following. He sets an example for others to follow, he listens and cares. Following is an option. *(Minirth Meier Clinic, Radio 74, April 1997)*

Leadership is only evident in the response of the followers. If the followers lack confidence or trust in their leader, or show any kind of animosity towards him, or are not inspired by him, then the so-called leader is not a leader. He may still have power and authority over the group, but he is a flawed leader, with potential for the group's failure in spite of his management skills. A leader without followers is a contradiction. So is an imposed or installed leader (which is why many so-called leaders are not leaders at all). Leadership is a two-way relationship, created jointly by the leader and the followership, and cannot be ordained from above.

> The functioning capability developed and applied by people and organisations is largely the result of the process of leading. Most people will not go further or faster or deeper than the leader will take them; the

group is enabled or limited by the leader. *(Organisational Effectiveness)*

Followership prevents imposture. A would-be leader whose leadership behaviours are not yet fully developed cannot deceive his followers, who recognise his deceit and cease to follow him, or follow with caution. Dishonest behaviour discourages and disheartens them.

Loyalty, so easily misplaced, is too easy an option for the followers. In its turn, unearned loyalty brings little to the leader. Unswerving devotion to him as an individual is cloying, burdensome and without value. If the leader earns and deserves loyalty, members of the group will behave positively to achieve the goals he has set. If, on the other hand, the leader doesn't merit loyalty from group members, their allegiance to him is misplaced. They might swear allegiance to the leader, only to find themselves committed to actions and goals that, at best, they are uncomfortable with or, at worst, they cannot in conscience perform.

Losing Followers

Followers can be enticed away by other leaders, even if the group's allegiances are thereby called into question. This is not a matter of fickle nature; it is quite normal and natural for people to follow the leader who offers most in the way of inspiration, reward and fulfilment. This can happen even in the most hierarchical of organisations. An employee may, for example, be subordinate to one manager but may see another manager as a role model, as a person who stimulates and inspires and is worth following. Or a follower may become disillusioned, and actively seek out another leader to follow.

Either way, the effective manager-as-leader knows, or learns, how to regain the group member's trust. He observes, questions, ruminates, discusses – and takes small steps to re-establish his role as leader. What the effective leader will not do is threaten, over-promise and use his power to "bring the offender back into line." He creates challenges, confirms the direction and tasks of the group, delegates responsibility – and takes a good look at his own performance as leader, with the aim of improving his leadership behaviour.

On their side, followers are not expected to display loyalty in the face of flawed leadership. Group members *are* expected to show that they are trustworthy and that they accept delegated projects, but they need not shrink from voicing their opinion of the leader in his various leadership roles. They may speak to him of his failings, and even suggest ways of improving his performance, offering "behaviour-sharpening" guidelines such as those described in this book. On the other hand, a group member can demonstrate his belief in the leader's qualities by delegating upwards, by inviting the leader to handle some task that he is ill equipped or too loaded to handle himself. Effective followers view their leader as a resource.

> A leader is like a shepherd. He stays behind the flock, letting the most nimble go out ahead, whereupon the others follow, not realising that all along they are being directed from behind. *(Nelson Mandela)*

Transferring leadership

A leader can transfer his leadership talents to a new group, in the same way that a professional manager can use his skills in a new environment. But, since leadership doesn't exist without followership, the leader can only be effective when the new group of followers accepts his behaviour as leader. This involves a forming/norming/storming/performing process, in which the new leader has to prove himself by offering his credentials (the Eleven Roles), displaying affinity with the group, meeting and defeating resistance, and finally being accepted as leader by the group. The group itself, wary of the newcomer, nevertheless has a duty to remain open to change. Members must accept that a new leader brings different cultural baggage with him, and that he will want to make changes, some immediate, some longer-term, thus consolidating his leadership. Negotiation and compromise may be necessary.

> People follow leaders not just for what they do, but out of respect for what they are. *(The Leadership Trust, UK)*

Sharpen your "Followership" behaviour

- Respect and trust your leader.
- Challenge your leader's visions. Make him uncomfortable with his strategies. Try to share his decisions.
- Tell the leader your concerns, your ideas for innovation. You have a duty to contribute to the group's progress.
- Be trustworthy. Don't cheat your leader.
- Delegate upwards. Treat your leader as a resource.
- Recognise that you are as much an ambassador of the group as the leader is.

The Eleven Roles of the Leader

There is little doubt that there is some capacity for leadership within practically every one of us. However, like every skill, the capacity to lead comes with experience and study. We can only improve ourselves, in any way, by a conscious effort to learn how to do better. *(Sir John Harvey-Jones)*

Let's see how patterns of leadership behaviour can be analysed, and separated into distinct components, in a way that enables us to identify means by which leaders' performance (as leaders) can be measured and improved.

In my observation, leadership comprises eleven major Roles, with a number of minor traits complementing the major ones. Each one of the eleven is necessary to achieve the common task, to drive and to inspire, a Role for the leader to adopt according to the situation. Each Role is expected, even demanded, by group members.

Every leader has to play a part from time to time, a part which, like an actor's, doesn't come naturally or easily. But the skill he shows in playing the part – the Role – makes the difference between effective leadership and failure in achieving the heartfelt attention of the followers. However, the leader can adopt each Role to a greater or lesser degree, and therefore has the potential for leadership, provided that the adopted Roles which are dominant are appropriate to the task. The following chapters offer encouragement and advice in the development and adoption of each Role.

In summary, these are the Eleven Roles of the Leader. Each is more fully described in the following pages.

1. The Challenger

Speaking up to question the form of change, its direction and its implementation is essential for the group's effectiveness. Acceptance is too easy. A manager's unilateral decisions should be challenged; he may have misjudged the feelings, the competence or the capability of the group. The manager-as-leader questions his own decisions, and the actions of others, with 'Five Whys and a How.' Challenge is the first manifestation of an individual's leadership potential.

2. The Pilot

The leader pilots the group's endeavours towards the goal which he had envisioned (created) – the 'could-be' future state. A plan for achieving the goal is essential. The leader-as-pilot communicates the vision and the plan persuasively, using his preferred style, and encourages creativity and vision in others.

3. The Transformer

Change is all there is, and change cannot happen without leadership. Leadership flourishes when change (transformation) is a leap, not a step. Different kinds of change require different approaches, but all of them mean pain, sometimes rejection. The leader prepares for resistance to change. He uses risk to highlight the benefits of change. He expresses optimism in the outcome, but values failure and plans for it.

4. The Judge (of Risk)

Risk can be welcomed and used to drive change. Risk involves judgement: failure can be planned for. Optimism generates energy, but beware of too much of it.

5. The Communicator

Perception of the leader is influenced by how he communicates. The most effective communication is face-to-face, direct, concise and careful. But the leader also writes with care and precision. He addresses audiences with skill, handles meetings effectively and listens well.

6. Mister Trustful

If he doesn't trust his followers, a leader is not a leader. Trust needs courage; it's difficult, precarious and reciprocal. Trust boosts morale, cuts down the need for supervision and encourages initiative.

7. The Delegator

The loneliness of leadership is eased through trust and through delegation, done properly and well. Successful sharing of tasks and projects includes evaluation of the situation and of the delegate(s), handing over authority with responsibility (but not accountability), self-control on the part of the leader, monitoring the process and learning from failure.

8. The Rock

Steady as a Rock, the leader demonstrates dependability, trustworthiness and integrity, as well as proof of competence, high principles and strong convictions. He under-promises and over-delivers, doesn't shrink from expressing doubt, and takes time to think.

9. The Hero

With increasing competition from popular heroes, the leader accepts his responsibility to be looked up to and to be emulated. He puts effort into visible exemplary behaviour.

10. The Self-Manager

Self-confidence combined with humility enhances the leader's managerial competence. He knows and exploits his strengths, corrects his weaknesses, exercises self-control and uses self-doubt to challenge his own behaviour.

11. The Coach

Leaders are created in different ways, but leadership behaviour is developed through experience and practice: others can give a helping hand. The leader helps people (including his successor) to develop through his own behaviour, encouragement and formal programmes.

What others have written

Bill Drath and **Chuck Palus** see the purpose of leadership as making sense and making meaning, rather than influencing or decision-making. Leadership helps people to make sense of what they are doing, so that they understand and are committed. In this way, leadership becomes a community-specific process; authority is one of a number of tools used to create meaning. The leader communicates the vision by touching the hearts of others. Influence is the outcome of leadership, not its essence. Leadership is about what people do together.

Leadership is the art of bringing out the best in people – getting average people to perform consistently in an outstanding manner. *(Ed Woolard, former CEO of DuPont)*

1. The Challenger

Speaking up to question the form of change, its direction and its implementation is essential for the group's effectiveness. Acceptance is too easy. A manager's unilateral decisions should be challenged; he may have misjudged the feelings, the competence or the capability of the group. The manager-as-leader questions his own decisions, and the actions of others, with 'Five Whys and a How.' Challenge is the first manifestation of an individual's leadership potential.

A group needs someone to speak up when change is being planned, when risks are being taken. The direction which the change will take, its form and its content, should be the subject of challenge, scrutiny and debate, of revision and modification. However, the autocratic form of many companies, public services and even of some voluntary organisations makes little or no allowance for discussion or consideration by the people who will be affected by the change, or by those who will have to implement it.

In the business world, managers have long been used to taking unilateral decisions on strategy and tactics. They claim that there isn't time for discussion, or that their reports have neither the competence nor even the inclination to give such issues their attention and to challenge the wisdom of their managers' decisions.

An effective manager knows his group, its ways of working, its motivations and its capabilities. As a consequence, his assertive decisions and actions take into account the needs and proficiencies of group members. But not all managers have such skill, nor do some managers have the opportunity to ascertain what each member of the group expects and can contribute. So the manager's decisions may be expedient, misunderstood, resented and, even worse, obstructed by individuals in the group.

Give the manager a leadership role, with the behavioural skills that we are describing, and his strategic or tactical decisions stand a chance of being accepted more readily. Alternatively, he confers with all or some members of the group to ensure that the eventual decision will be accepted and be acted on. This is the opportunity for group members to express their doubts, to question and challenge courageously at each stage of the decision-making process, and to offer their own alternatives, in a nonadversarial way.

Challenge is often the first manifestation of latent leadership. When someone questions, "Why are we doing (this)?" and goes on with "Wouldn't it be better if we did it (that way)?" then an aspiring leader is showing his mettle. A leader makes people uncomfortable about the status quo.

> Difference of opinion leads to inquiry, and inquiry leads to truth.
> *(Thomas Jefferson)*

Note that it is the idea that is challenged, not the person. Saying, "You are stupid to propose this idea" raises hackles and creates conflict. A neutrally phrased challenge, with ownership, gives an opportunity for dialogue: "Your idea has merits, but I'm not sure that it's the best way forward."

A manager is as much a follower as his subordinates are. He is on the receiving end of many inputs – proposals, decisions, actions, orders – from those he reports to. It's easy for him, as a subordinate and follower, to accept these inputs. After all, he says, his bosses know what they're doing, don't they? And there isn't time to question every proposal and order, is there? There are too many other fires to fight, aren't there? Acceptance is undemanding, trouble-free. It allows time and energy for the daily round of managerial tasks and interruptions. And, if the input causes outrage, it provides the (often welcome) opportunity to vent one's feelings in private about those 'stupid people upstairs'. This unquestioning attitude is contagious. It is easily adopted by group members, with the result that bad decisions may be made and bad plans put into action.

Five Whys and a How

Seeing the issue in the context of the big picture and thinking it through, taking it to pieces and seeing whether the components fit together well, and giving thought to all the likely results and ramifications – these are the actions of a leader. They require effort and courage. He makes the effort to question every decision he himself takes, and courage takes him down the same road when confronted with the decisions of others. First he asks the right questions, and listens to the answers. He confers with colleagues. He researches previous experience, to seek ways in which others have done the same thing. Then he challenges every notion, first within his own mind, to be sure that he understands all the issues involved, and all the options for solution that are available. Then, if he believes that there's a better way than the one proposed, he argues his case – persuasively, with caution (because he may not have all the facts at his disposal) and with conviction.

> *A factory manager noticed a crate lying apart from other crates. He asked why, and was told that it contained rejects. "Why?" "The machine making them developed a fault." "Why?" "The machine hasn't been maintained according to schedule, and the indexing set has got a few micrometres out of sync." "Why has the maintenance schedule not been observed?" "The new machine operator hasn't been told to signal the need for a service break on the machine." "How does the work team plan to correct this situation?" The answer was, of course, additional training. This process of getting to the root of a problem, and of seeking a solution to it, is known as 'Five Whys and a How.'*

Be aware that challenge is not cynicism, the attitude of distrust and disbelief that is common among educated people today. Today's cynicism is as easy to adopt as riding a bicycle, but has no relationship to the challenge that creates value, or the questioning that brings new ideas to the table. Challenge, to have value, must be backed by honest inquiry, constructive determination to excel, and a mind open to reason and innovation.

Challenge may have negative aspects. It can underline indecision, an inability to firmly make up one's mind. It may accentuate doubt in oneself or in others. Questioning can cause useless delay through ignorance or for nefarious reasons. Questions of a certain kind ("Can you assure us that...?") are used to undermine confidence and authority. None of these behaviours is that of a leader, or of a group member dedicated to the achievement of the group's goals.

> A little rebellion now and then is a good thing. *(Thomas Jefferson)*

Sharpen your behaviour as a Challenger

- Don't hesitate to challenge paradigms, conventions and orthodoxy.
- When you are the challenger, offer your own (alternative) ideas clearly, with ownership, with conviction, with substantiation and with an open mind.
- Put the short-term in the context of the long-term. Ask, "Why are you/we doing this? What is its contribution to the strategy?"
- Challenge the idea, not the person.
- Stimulate thinking in others: ask 'Five Whys and a How.'
- Think ideas through, your own and others'. What could be the consequences?

Who could be affected – which stakeholder, which competitor, where, when?
- What are the alternatives? What might happen if we didn't go ahead?
- Don't accept the opinions of others without examining them carefully
- And when you are being challenged:
    - listen and understand
    - remember that your own ideas and actions may be inappropriate, and that better ones probably exist
    - don't use any of the many forms of rejection* until you are absolutely sure that your proposal is the best.

* Here are some that you've heard:
"*We tried it before, and it didn't work*"
"*It costs too much*"
"*We don't have the time*"
"*Why change it if it's working OK?*"
"*It isn't in the budget*"
"*Top management will never go for it*"
"*Let's set up a working group to study it*"
"*Can you guarantee it'll work?*"
"*It's against policy*"

2. The Pilot

The leader pilots the group's endeavours towards the goal which he had envisioned (created) – the 'could-be' future state. A plan for achieving the goal is essential. The leader-as-pilot communicates the vision and the plan persuasively, using his preferred style, and encourages creativity and vision in others.

Strategic planning is a key component of most managers' work. A manager must look far forward to plan his courses of action, his resources, and the eventualities that might upset these plans. But as leader his mind is fixed on a specific goal, a well-defined vision of the ideal state for the group, the 'should-be' state – or even of a state which might never exist, the dream, the 'could-be' state. His vision is creative, audacious, even (to start with) unbelievable. He studies his imagined state and refines it over time, to give it substance within the bounds of possibility. He uses his knowledge of the present situation to determine the difference between the here-and-now and the envisioned future state, and the effort and resources needed to accomplish the change. He redesigns his vision continuously as conditions alter and as the goal is approached. He shifts direction only under extreme external pressure.

Manfred F. R. Kets de Vries tells us, "*Make a vision exciting: it must identify an enemy, stretch quality, offer an exciting (inviting) future, create a sense of pride, and go well beyond bottom-line concerns. It must be communicated (well), involve people, have immediate relevance and be action-oriented.*" To this we can add: a vision must stretch the capabilities of the group's resources (Browning's "A man's reach should exceed his grasp"), and it must be finite – there must be a light at the end of the tunnel.

Once he is happy with it, the leader-as-visionary pilots the group towards his vision. He does this either in an assertive style, brooking little or no argument, or co-operatively, allowing the group to modify the leader's ideas. (More on this in 'Leadership Styles' on page 5.) If he chooses to adopt the co-operative style, the leader is aware of the pitfalls of consultation. Too little input, and the group's buy-in is limited, even non-existent. Too much, and the issue may be watered down, full of compromise and fudge. And consultation means listening to, and acting upon, others' views with which one may not whole-heartedly agree. We have all known cases where, having asked someone's advice, we ignored it and consequently had to deal with a sullen, unco-operative person.

A leader (is someone who) is able to develop and communicate a vision which gives meaning to the work of others. *(Charles B. Handy)*

Creating a Vision

Imagination is more important than knowledge. *(Albert Einstein)*

The leader doesn't wait for opportunities – he creates them. He knows that what seems impossible may simply be untried. He is creative in the sense that his strategic thinking, based on

- analysis of the present situation
- imagination and inventiveness
- confidence in his view of the future
- understanding of the risks involved

gives him the strength to propose a direction for change that the group can accept with enthusiasm. His creativity extends to looking outside his field of experience, his speciality, his organisation. He steals the good ideas of others. He invites others to contribute their ideas. But he takes care to avoid letting personal ambition (his or others') influence the group's future. In fact he recognises that his future and the group's future may lie in different directions.

The creation of a vision, its assertive communication to the group and the group's acceptance of it affect the group's confidence in the leader, and confidence of its own success. This is especially true if the group takes ownership for the democratic development of the vision and the plan to make it happen. Either way the leader, in his turn, has confidence that the group has accepted the vision as a goal, and that group members will make every effort to achieve that goal.

Nobody can lead unless he has the gift of vision and the desire in his soul to leave things in the world a little better than he found them. He will strive for something which may appear unattainable, but which he believes in his heart can one day be reached, if not by him, by his successors, if he can help to pave the way. *(HM King George VI)*

The Plan

Vision is not the same as planning. Planning is a vital part of the manager's function, where 'planning is more important than the plan.' But while the manager uses a road map to plan a course for the group, the leader-as-guide maintains direction by using a chart and a compass. He imparts his vision, the distant horizon, to the group so that they understand where they are going, and why. And here we come to a 'bifocal' behaviour of the manager-as-leader. A manager must be able to see not only the direction (as leader) but also the route (as manager) along which he will guide the group to reach the envisioned goal.

The leader knows that the group must be shifted from the present set of paradigms to a new environment. In creating his vision, therefore, his plan and the strategy for accomplishing it include

- the direction to be taken
- the resources needed
- monitoring and evaluation
- provision for contingencies.

> Plans do not need to include a vision. *(John P. Kotter)*. [But they do need a goal, a desired outcome, something to aim for.]

It is a myth that plans stifle creativity. Some say that a plan sets the action in concrete, that nothing can be changed. But the people who have to take action need a plan to give them the direction, the timing, the resources needed and available, the 'what-ifs' and the expected outcome. Preparing a plan that takes account of all these factors, and achieving commitment to it, demands the highest degree of creativity. This is the only guarantee of success. Have you ever been set a goal with no plan? Where improvisation and seat-of-the-pants expediency rule? Was it successful?

> Chance favours only the mind that is prepared. *(Louis Pasteur)*

The leader's charted course to the envisioned state (his plan of action) can be achieved using one of two leadership styles, authoritarian or democratic (more about this in 'Leadership Styles' where I have preferred 'assertive' to 'authoritarian'). The assertive style involves the way that an artist draws a straight line. You and I use a ruler, but an artist will draw an equally straight line freehand. How does he do it? He puts the point of his pencil on A, then fixes his eyes on B and moves the pencil. The result is a perfectly straight line joining A and B. (Try it!) The assertive leader does the same thing. He uses the present situation as the starting point and, fixing his gaze on the distant point that he wants the group to reach, draws up a course of action. The result is the direct path along which the leader can guide the group to achieve that goal. As the group approaches its goal, the leader lifts his sights and broadens his view to encompass a new horizon. He refocuses on a new goal, and charts a new course towards it.

Alternatively, the co-operative (democratic) style is to invite the group to plan its own path forward. More on this on page 116, under 'Creative Problem Solving.'

Whichever style the leader chooses, assertive or co-operative, he involves all the people included in the plan. People are readier to accept changes which they feel they have helped to create. (And we are readier to reject change if it's someone else's idea.) So, if the leader has chosen the assertive style, he will enthusiastically communicate his vision to the group, emphasising the risks if his plan is not adopted. He will set the criteria for performance. He may invite comment. If, on the other hand, the co-operative style is selected, the whole process, from the here-and-now to the envisioned state, plus the plan to accomplish successful change, is up for discussion and refinement, with every member of the group (maybe others, too) contributing.

So much for the leader's vision. What about encouraging vision in others? An effective leader stimulates innovation, invites creativity and encourages ideas. He welcomes strategic thinking and reflections on change and improvement. He provokes competition between ideas (but not between their creators). He gives credit when someone else's idea is adopted; he uses tact when rejecting an idea that won't work.

> Some men see things as they are and ask *Why?* Others dream things that never were and ask *Why not? (George Bernard Shaw)*

What others have written

J. M. Stewart lists six steps in creating a vision for the business:
1. view the future and present states through each stakeholder's eyes
2. develop a broad description of the likely future environment
3. create a vision of what the organisation could be
4. contrast the future vision with the present state
5. express the values that will guide the organisation towards its vision
6. ensure that the vision is expressed in terms of actionable concepts.

Sir John Harvey-Jones writes that the vision is best generated if those involved have a high degree of mutual respect, tolerance and humour.

Roger Gill of the Leadership Trust reminds us of research that suggests seven attributes of an effective vision:

1. brevity
2. clarity
3. abstractness
4. challenge
5. future orientation
6. stability
7. desirability, or ability to inspire

Of these the first, third and seventh appear to be particularly important where growth is concerned.

Begin with the end in mind. *(Stephen R. Covey)*

Sharpen your behaviour as a Pilot

- Take time to think broadly, long-term, about the purpose (mission) of the group. Dream of the ideal state of the organisation. Keep your personal ambition separate.
- Create. Use your dreams to build a future for the group, creating robust opportunities for success which demand strenuous efforts to achieve.
- Copy, plagiarise, take a leaf out of others' books. Seek out the successful, identify the reasons for success and copy them.
- Are the resources – time, money, manpower, materials, accommodation – available? Now and in the future? If you foresee a shortfall, create an opportunity for correcting it.
- If you choose the assertive style when your vision is clear to you (though not unchangeable), identify the difference between the here-and-now and your could-be state, and list the steps and resources needed to accomplish the change and to monitor progress. Decide how, and to whom, to communicate your vision.
- If you choose the co-operative route, tell the group confidently about your vision. Invite the group to challenge it. Be ready to accept changes. Once the group has modified your vision to its own (and your) satisfaction, invite the members to list the steps and resources needed to accomplish the change and to monitor progress.

3. The Transformer

Change is all there is, and change cannot happen without leadership. Leadership flourishes when transformation is a leap, not a step. Different kinds of change require different approaches, but all mean pain, sometimes rejection. The leader prepares for resistance to change. He uses risk to highlight the benefits of change. He expresses optimism in the outcome, but values failure and plans for it.

Change – or transition, or transformation – from one state to another is an accepted and integral part of today's society. Restructuring, innovation, growth, make-over, even progress – call it what you like, instability is a permanent feature of everyone's life. Transformation is seen as essential for survival of the individual, of the organisation, and even of society.

Change cannot happen without leadership. It needs a leader to create the opportunities for change, to anticipate change, and to plan for it. And the corollary is that leadership flourishes in times of change. Whenever and wherever change is called for, the leader takes the group through the change process, and carries the burden of change. Change throws down a challenge which must be met in order to allow the system to continue to function. Meeting this challenge demands the creativity of leadership.

Change may originate with

- the leader, whose vision may (usually does) involve creative change
- a group member, employee, customer, supplier or an asset (a building, a machine)
- senior management, the club committee, the government
- competition or legislation
- market change or new technology.

Leaders welcome change and many managers have the skills to prove themselves leaders in the process of change. But some managers find it difficult to adopt appropriate behaviour. It is in times of change that managers' leadership behaviour can be examined, and steps taken to develop it to ensure the success of the transformation process which is taking place.

Mastering change involves a clear vision of the 'should-be' or 'could-be' state compared with the present state. Mastering change also involves an occasional look over the shoulder, particularly during the change process. The effective leader has a sense of history and of continuity. He understands the value of corporate memory and learns from the past. He takes care to repeat the successes, and to avoid repeating the failures.

> Make change happen before it grabs you by the throat. *(John Adair)*

Change, to be effectively accomplished, demands consistency of communication (written, oral, decision-making) by all drivers of change (managers and leaders). People affected by change will naturally look for the weaknesses: lack of whole-hearted commitment by management, watering-down of resolution, changes of direction that give them hope for reversal of the decision to change. They seek every opportunity for maintenance of the status quo. So, together, all the drivers of change must demonstrate full commitment in their communications. They must display enthusiasm and optimism. They must be one step ahead of the rest in their dedication to the benefits that the change will bring. They must recognise that short-term and visible results are necessary for the change to be seen as inevitable and beneficial.

> If you don't have inspirational leadership you will never have successful change. *(James Strachan, Audit Commission chairman 2005)*

Kinds of transformation

Change, the disruption of the status quo, can be many things. It can mean improvement or refocusing or retrenchment. Change can be voluntary (created by the group or its leader) or involuntary (caused by outside influences). Change can be short-term or long-term, can be major (merger, take-over) or minor (change of letterhead). Change can be ordained ("You will do this differently") or offered ("If you agree, this is how we might do it better").

It involves, as part of the predictable 'should-be' future expectations of the organisation,

- the growth
- the resources and the ways in which they are organised
- the reaction to predictable future influences.

Alternatively, change towards the vision, the 'could-be' image, describes the more challenging path towards the best possible future for the organisation, an ideal state.

External influences, for good and ill, are taken into account, though some of them can be seized as opportunities rather than confronted as problems.

> Leadership is the use of power to effect positive change. *(Marlene Caroselli)*

People will not go further or faster than the leader takes them, so the leader's task in the change process is to go as far and as fast as the group can and will follow. The leader sets objectives for each stage of the change process, with tough goals and short deadlines. He creates and maintains a sense of urgency. He recognises that a relationship-oriented leadership style, as described by F. E. Fiedler, is essential for successful change, rather than a task-oriented style, which discourages innovative thinking and the attitude of challenge that generates ideas.

> Successful change needs time, compassion and readiness to shoulder the responsibility for the action. *(Sir John Harvey-Jones)*

Change means pain

> If you want to make enemies, try to change something. *(Woodrow Wilson)*

Whatever kind of transformation is envisioned, it will be painful. But the pain of change also generates creativity and the energy to press forward. Thus once the need for, and benefits of, change have been accepted (often the most difficult part of the change process), the group and its leader will find the inner resources to handle the change process in the most effective and beneficial way.

Voluntary improvement is easiest to handle and the least painful, with its obvious benefits and the fact that ownership is within the group. Involuntary change which involves refocusing on a new goal can be accepted, though reluctantly, since the people involved have to re-orient themselves in the new situation. The comfort factor disappears temporarily. But a major change which involves loss of job, status or confidence causes anger, frustration and depression – even among those not directly affected, and even if the change is a voluntary one.

Change affects individuals in different ways, either because of their personality or because of the nature of the change itself. A minor change to Jane's work-role can affect John's work-role more dramatically, and be taken much more seriously by John. The leader knows that he must expect selfishness and short-sightedness when a

43

change is proposed. He is prepared for the worst. Change induces fear, so the leader tackles it first and says, "Follow me."

A leader dealing with change is prepared for resistance and reaction. To ease the process, he starts by gently unfreezing the existing situation, undermining the status quo and establishing the need for change. He lays out the current position, explaining its drawbacks. He uses benchmarks to erode complacency. He invites criticism of the ways things are. He generates creative tension (not emotional tension) by creating discomfort with the status quo. This generates high productivity and reduces resistance to change.

> Progress is impossible without change, and those who cannot change
> their minds cannot change anything. *(George Bernard Shaw)*

Once the group has accepted the need for change, he can start the implementation of the change process. He tables the options, the different ways in which the current situation can be transformed. He either (co-operatively) invites discussion and eventual agreement on the path forward, or he (assertively) tells the group which option he has decided on, together with the plan of action (which he may co-operatively table for comment and agreement). Communication skills, concern for people and integrity are vital.

The leader initiates the change process by ensuring that everyone knows the first steps to be taken. If they don't, frustration will be the first obstacle to overcome. Then, with the group engaged on the change process, the leader monitors and evaluates the use of resources – the time spent, the funding, the energy – and ensures that the good relationship of the group with external influences is maintained. He uses his managerial skills and authority to clear away obstacles, to smooth the path and to facilitate the group's progress towards each short-term goal. He inspires group members to do the same. He encourages risk-taking.

The leader creates opportunities for short-term positive results ('wins') to keep up morale and momentum. He allows these wins to be celebrated, but he doesn't declare victory until the vision is accomplished. The leader exploits short-term wins as springboards to change systems and procedures, and to re-state the new policies that are linked to the vision.

Finally, with the transformation completed, he refreezes the new situation and consolidates the change. He invites discussion, inside and outside the group, with a view to getting the last ounce of benefit out of the change. He benchmarks against the plan. He starts planning for the next step.

The price of progress is the pain of change. (Tom Hopkins)

What others have written

John Kotter tells us what managers do when implementing change:

- Create a sense of urgency
- Put together a strong team
- Create an appropriate vision
- Communicate the vision broadly
- Empower champions of change
- Produce sufficient short-term results to give their efforts credibility
- Build momentum, and use it to tackle tougher change
- Anchor the new behaviour in organisational culture.

Robert Kelley suggests that there are five points of view when looking at the effects of change (his 'Five Cs'):

- Colleagues: borrow and test others' ideas, get others' insights
- Company: its visions and values
- Customers: an important, often overlooked, stakeholder
- Competition: what will be its reaction?
- Creativity: the could-be, the dream (the plan).

John Burdett identifies ten ways to generate creative tension:

1. Benchmarking against the best.
2. Moving the culture from recognising seniority to recognising merit.
3. Improving the quality of performance feedback to include both peers and subordinates (i.e., 360 degree).
4. Removing those who represent poor role models.
5. Encouraging risk.
6. Taking non-decision-making levels out of the hierarchy.
7. Rewarding success.
8. Destroying restrictive concepts of turf.
9. Striving for synergies.

10. Focusing on outputs.

John W. Hunt offers six ingredients for success in the change process:
1. felt pressure for change
2. direction and power
3. leadership and vision
4. capacity to learn the new behaviours or procedures
5. actionable first steps
6. rewards that are relevant to those concerned.

R. J. Marshak stresses the need to use language that is appropriate to the type of change.

Sir John Harvey-Jones writes that, to understand the need for change, people must be made aware of the risks in not changing.

Douglas Ready's research led him to the conclusion that transformation is a regenerative process, not a one-time event, and it is not optional.

Roger Harrison's view is that the leader needs to be visible, leading change from the top.

Warren Bennis sets out eight success factors for leading change:
1. managing the dream
2. embracing error
3. encouraging reflective backtalk and dissent
4. demonstrating optimism and faith
5. understanding that people can grow
6. seeing the long-term view
7. understanding stakeholder symmetry
8. creating strategic alliances

Sharpen your behaviour as a Transformer

- Establish the reasons for change. Describe the defects of the present situation to the group. Lay out the benefits of change, and its drawbacks, and how to handle both.

- Set objectives for the new situation: goals, deadlines. Create urgency.
- Collect data. Ask the people involved in the change for their ideas, opinions, suggestions, objections. Act devil's advocate: challenge, question – and suggest more improvements.
- Predict the problems. Invite individuals to list first the positive aspects of the change, then the possible resistance and reaction and ways of counteracting them.
- Decide how you want to plan the change process. Use the assertive or co-operative stages of the CPS process (page 116).
- Identify the new/additional resources required, their availability, possible shortfalls and how to overcome them.
- Plan the implementation of the change – timing, fading out the old while introducing the new, retraining, restructuring.
- Keep the transition time short. Aim for all the people involved knowing everything on the first day.
- Communicate the plan to everyone involved, inside and outside the group. Show enthusiasm and determination. The first reaction to change is nearly always adverse. Be prepared for negative feelings; acknowledge them but stick to your guns. Lead the process.
- Make sure that the resources – time, money, manpower, accommodation – are available. Now and in the future.
- Emphasise the benefits, justify the drawbacks of the new situation. Detail the risks, explain how problems will be overcome. Explain why some ideas and suggestions were not adopted.
- Ensure that each group member knows his new role and is qualified (trained) to cope with it.
- As the process moves forward, monitor, check, rectify faults. Evaluate the results.

4. The Judge (of Risk)

Risk can be welcomed and used to drive change. Risk involves judgement: failure can be planned for. Optimism generates energy, but beware of too much of it.

The leader is not afraid of innovation and the unknown. He understands risk, and can judge the timing for prudent risk-taking in the cause of change. He shares with his group not only his vision but also the risks that he sees, in a co-operative style if he thinks fit, so that the group can commit to the risks before the balloon goes up.

The leader uses risk as a tool to highlight the value of change to the group. He says, "If we don't change, this (unacceptable) situation will arise." He does not attempt to calculate the risk, although he does try to assess the effects of risk-taking; what might happen if we do versus what might happen if we don't. But in laying out, for himself and the rest of the group, the risk and its possible results, he aims for the best possible outcome. He expresses optimism and doesn't go for half measures *("We'll just put the male animals in the Ark for now, and see how we get on. The females can be loaded later.")*.

Sometimes the risk lies in not taking a risk. Sometimes the biggest risk lies in not making a big enough move, a breakthrough rather than an incremental step. Courage, as well as sound judgement of risk, is required.

> Accept the unknown as a friend, not as an enemy. (*Bertrand Piccard, interviewed on Swiss television*)

An effective leader uses good judgement. He knows when to be assertive, to make haste, to overrule objections, to cut corners. He knows when to cut his losses. He understands the value-in-necessity of leaving an investment, of shrugging his shoulders and starting afresh. He takes account of the risk involved in these practices when making his decisions, as he does with every decision he makes.

Plan for Failure

Leaders value failure as useful experience from which to draw lessons for future plans and actions. No blame, no shame – as long as the rules have been followed. The rules are

- up-front acknowledgement by all group members that risk is involved
- acceptance of the cost of possible failure, in terms of expense and loss of progress towards the goal.

> When a young executive at IBM lost the company $30,000 on an experiment that did not come off, he expected to be fired. But Thomas Watson, the company's founder, had different ideas. "Why would I fire you?" he asked. "We've spent $30,000 educating you." *(Anon)*

Optimism is the key to the can-do spirit, to the don't-take-no-for-an-answer attitude to resistance that is essential to all executive leadership. Over-optimism, on the other hand, can over-state the potential for a positive result, and result in disappointment.

> It is a crime to despair. *(Winston Churchill)*

Sharpen your behaviour as a Judge of Risk

- Share it. Use risk to emphasise the value of change.
- Study all the risk factors: the people, the events, the external influences, everything that can make the process unreliable and lead to failure. Weigh up the factors, balance them; then take the route that your intuition tells you to. The data feed the decision, they don't make it.
- Be optimistic, yet bi-focal. View success and failure as equal possibilities. Don't fear failure but plan for it.
- Turn risk into opportunity. Think positively and creatively about taking advantage of the factors outside your control (shortages of resources – weather – new competition – changes in markets – legislation – technology).

5. The Communicator

Perception of the leader is influenced by how he communicates. The most effective communication is face-to-face, direct, concise and careful. But the leader also writes with care and precision. He addresses audiences with skill, handles meetings effectively and listens well.

It has been said that the only output of a manager is communication. Yes – and of the leader too. The content of his communication – what he writes and says – is important, and this is emphasised in the other chapters of this book. In this chapter, however, it is his style, the manner in which he communicates his message, that we deal with – how he says it and how he writes it. And how he receives messages from others.

Nothing influences others' perception of a leader more quickly and lastingly than the way in which he communicates. This chapter, therefore, should have a high priority for anyone aspiring to establish himself as a leader.

Communication is fundamental to the exercise of leadership. Without the ability to clearly express his vision and principles, to delegate tasks and to voice his challenges, an aspiring leader will not be recognised as one. He must be able to demonstrate trust, trustworthiness and other behaviours by words as well as by actions, and by listening as much as by speaking and writing.

Heading the list of communication tools is behaviour itself. A leader demonstrates and acts out his visions and principles in the way he behaves, consistently and without compromise. He walks the talk. He lives the values that he cherishes:

- He is a poet – articulate, a dreamer, a visionary.
- He is a story-teller, breathing life into the vision, helping others to understand what it means for them.
- He is a role player – an actor mouthing others' words, conscious of his "public".
- He is a disseminator of new ideas.
- He is a gatekeeper, a channel of communication, an arbitrator.
- He is an analyst, a strategist and tactician.

- He is a designer, understanding how the parts fit together; he sees inter-relationships and makes connections.

> The leader enacts the vision, walks the talk. *(Anon)*

A vital characteristic of effective communication is openness. The leader ensures that his listeners and readers know that he is holding back nothing of value, that he is showing all his cards. If others suspect that he is not being honest when communicating with them, they mistrust and even ignore or obstruct his messages. Another essential of effective communication is clarity. It is essential for a message to be understood by the recipient, and to be acted on in exactly the way in which the sender expects. A check for understanding is important, but more important is making sure in the first place that the message is unambiguous and complete.

> Communication, to be truly effective, relies on emotional intelligence for graphic impact, persuasive charm and memorability. *(Daniel Goleman)*

Face-to-face communication

The only truly effective communication is face-to-face, engaging emotional intelligence on both sides. It is only in situations where the listener and the speaker confront each other, with the opportunity for exchange of ideas, that perfect communication can take place. Not, however, that it always is perfect; there are many impediments to effective communication, such as lack of articulacy and an inability to listen properly and carefully, as well as barriers which can include hearing loss and lack of language skills. But if there is a choice between written and spoken communication, the latter must always take precedence if perfect understanding is desired.

In a manager/subordinate situation, this applies especially when change has to be communicated, whether it's for the individual alone or for the whole group. Alternatives, such as newsletters, posters, memos, videos, e-mail messages, even group meetings, are supplementary media, to be avoided as primary message-carriers because of their impersonal and non-interactive characteristics.

Effective face-to-face communication, in a hierarchical constituency such as a business, is always via one step of the hierarchy at a time. Thus the managing director cannot effectively communicate change to the machine operator – the speaker and the listener are on different wave-lengths, generating the potential for misunderstanding and mistrust. The only successful way of communicating change to the employee is from his supervisor, who in turn has been given all the details from his boss. The 'trickle-down' channel of communication, used with skill and success in the military, can be applied equally successfully to workplace situations. It can be adapted to 'trickle-up' too, for challenging and questioning.

With the flatter organisation, in which layers of management are kept to the minimum, the 'trickle-down' process has the advantage of allowing fast and effective communication, from top to bottom and from bottom to top. Where span of control is important (between 7 and 10 is considered as ideal for the number of people reporting to a manager), a large number of layers of management may result in slow, distorted and inefficient communication. In these circumstances, face-to-face communication is even more essential for ensuring that messages are understood.

Managements exist which, taking their cue from our modern media-driven society, use state-of-the-art communication tools to inform, and even confer with, large numbers of employees, shareholders, even customers. Inter-active television, video, e-mail, the Internet, even press and television interviews – all have been tried and found wanting when compared with face-to-face dialogue. But still they are used, and their users wonder why their messages meet with disbelief and scepticism.

The written and spoken word

Skill in communicating in speech and writing starts with an understanding of the needs and capabilities of others. The leader listens carefully to others in the group so that, when it is time to share his views and express his visions or his principles, he uses language that his listeners or readers can understand without ambiguity. He ensures that they follow his arguments by putting questions to them. If he suspects that there is doubt, he paraphrases his thoughts in a way that repeats the idea in a different form (mere repetition is usually unsuccessful). He challenges those who need to take action as a result of his communications, and refines his words to clarify doubts and misunderstandings.

> Short words are best and the old words when short are best of all.
> *(Winston Churchill)*

The leader uses simple language – short words, short sentences, a minimum of adjectives – in speech as well as in written communication. He inspires others to action, or to thinking, through economical use of emotional words and phrases. He structures his texts, to lead from the general to the particular, to present argument in a logical sequence, to meet likely doubts and misunderstandings. And, if there's a choice between saying it and writing it, he follows Lord Brabazon's advice: *"If you can't say it in twenty minutes, write it. "*

In every form of communication, the leader uses a sincere "we" rather than "I" or "you" when describing action to be taken. In this way, he confirms his membership of the group, and emphasises the cohesion of the people involved, including himself. But he asserts ownership of ideas and visions that originate with him (and acknowledges, of course, contributions made by others, especially members of the group he is leading). In fact, a leader expresses all his thoughts, feelings and opinions with ownership.

The leader uses clear, direct requests and directives. He doesn't suggest, hint, or prevaricate. When speaking, he doesn't start, "I'm sorry, but..." He makes his needs and wishes known without ambiguity. In particular, he says, "No" firmly, leaving no doubt of his meaning. He smiles. He sounds sincere. He exudes goodwill. People are happy to do what he asks of them.

He gives the listener time to respond when asking questions like "Have I made myself clear? Is there anything that I can add to help you understand?" He uses the trainer's trick of waiting seven seconds (an eternity!) for a response. He knows that this applies even more in a group situation than in the one-to-one discussion.

We have all experienced a moment of horror when we find that a letter or e-mail message which we have hurriedly written and sent turns out to be incomplete or ambiguous. Whenever possible, and especially for important messages, the leader allows twenty-four hours to elapse between writing and sending, with a final check just before putting the sheet into the envelope, or clicking on 'Send'. Of course this is not always practicable, but a few experiences in leaving and then returning to a written document will quickly convince anyone that re-reading and editing a document offer opportunities for improvement in expression and understanding that outweigh the hazards of delay. And the risk of delivering a message while under stress (angry, frustrated, euphoric, under time pressure) is minimised.

Preparation of important spoken messages also takes time. A speech or presentation takes at least six times longer to prepare than to make, while preparing and planning a meeting can take eight times longer than the meeting itself. A performance appraisal needs several hours of preparation by both parties, especially if the "No surprises" rule has not been observed. These lengthy preparation times reduce the risk of foul-ups resulting from omissions, false assumptions, surmise, guesswork and hasty conclusions.

What others have written

Howard Gardner writes that leadership (and followership) take place in the human mind. [Therefore communication (in both directions) is essential for effective leadership, in order to communicate the principles of the other ten Roles that leaders adopt to create and enable change.]

Rupert Eales-White expands on the theme of persuasion. He describes four styles:

1. use of logic
2. power of incentives
3. empathy
4. appeal to (the group's) norms and values.

In combination, they represent different levels of commitment to change:

1 + 2   the lowest level, effective only short-term

1 + 2 + 4   the next level, but still short-term

1 + 2 + 3 + 4   the highest level, a "voyage of discovery" for all concerned.

Roger Gill of the Leadership Trust, writing about communication of the vision, tells us that inspiring leaders craft their rhetoric:

*   they give examples, tell stories
*   they vary their speaking rhythms
*   they use familiar images, metaphors and analogies
*   they express hope and possibilities
*   they wax lyrical
*   they use repetition (Churchill's 'pile-driver – a tremendous whack')

Sharpen your behaviour as a Communicator

For the spoken word

*   take time to think things through. Prepare an important conversation or discussion well in advance, giving thought to the probable reaction of the other(s). Make notes and use them.
*   calm and thoughtful, never angry, no surprises. Don't deal with people when you are under stress (when you are emotionally ill-equipped to deal with the

situation).

- use moderate language always. Swallow your feelings.
- use language that the listener understands. Don't try to baffle or blind, or to score points by using high-flown terms.
- use emotional words and phrases, but frugally, to persuade and convince.
- check for understanding. Wait for answers (seven seconds!). Don't interrupt speech or thought. Listen carefully.
- when correcting or criticising, tell the good news first. Tell the listener what he or she has done that's good before you talk about the faulty behaviour. Never criticise personality (which can't be changed), only behaviour (which can).
- assert ownership of your thoughts. Don't say, "The only sensible policy is to match the competition." Instead say, "I believe that matching the competition is the best policy." Don't say, "Don't you think that we should postpone this for now?" but say, "I think that postponing discussion on this question would allow us time to collect more data."
- use direct language when asking. Not "Would you mind taking this to John?" but "Please take this to John." Don't suggest, "Why don't you ask John to help you?" but ask instead, "Please ask John to help you." Don't hint, "I need five copies of this for my meeting" but ask directly, "Please make five copies of this for my meeting." And smile!

For the written word

- put it in writing and keep it short.
- on paper or by e-mail, confirm everything of consequence – instructions, decisions, plans, reports, etc. – essential for clarity and understanding of both parties.
- use short words, concise phrases. Avoid jargon, 'officialese' and long-winded, bureaucratic language.
- leave important messages for 24 hours before sending them.

Presentations

We have all watched ambitious leaders make poor presentations, and watched them lose their impact as leaders. The worst were inaudible and disorganised, used their visual aids as notes (so that they continually turned to the screen), and refused to make eye contact with everyone in the audience. They didn't look or sound like leaders. They talked too long, without pausing, and their messages were unstructured. Some of them even read their speeches from a prepared text! (Remember how your mother read to you to send you to sleep?) Nothing, in fact, that a little training and practice could not have corrected, so that the other ten Roles of Leadership, in which they excelled, could shine and be recognised.

In addressing an audience, the Communicator remembers that he is highly visible when he is standing in front, and that, as a leader, he is judged as much on his style as on his message. The audience watches him as well as listening to him, and notes his body language – every move he makes with his hands, his feet, his whole body. (I was once one of 80 people addressed by a senior manager for 20 minutes. None of us heard his message because, throughout his talk, Jeff kept one hand in a trouser pocket and jingled coins. Nervousness?)

Research has shown that 7 per cent of a message is received verbally, 93 per cent non-verbally. Body language is a vital communications tool, whether in platform presentation or in one-to-one interpersonal communication. A lot of web sites describe body language well, and for reasons of space we'll limit ourselves to just three important points:

- face (especially eyes and eyebrows/forehead, which energetically display emotion) is the key element
- on the platform, hands convey more emotion and emphasis than most people realise
- waving arms about, and similar gestures, add emphasis.

Sharpen your behaviour when Presenting

- The more effort you put into preparing your presentation, the more effort your audience will put into listening to it. Preparation takes at least six times longer than the presentation itself.

    It usually takes more than three weeks to prepare a good impromptu speech. *(Mark Twain)*

- When preparing a presentation, think of a good beginning, work out a good ending, then find the shortest route between them.

    If you haven't struck oil in your first three minutes, stop boring! *(George Jessel)*

- Put your message clearly, with logical sequence and no irrelevant digressions.
- Know your audience's needs, desires, language, attitude.

- Decide what you want to achieve: learning, discussion, problem-solving, feedback, action, persuasion,..
- Check the room and the equipment long before your start time.
- If some of the audience don't know you, introduce yourself by name, and then state the subject of your presentation. Include your credentials – your authority to speak on the subject.
- Tell the audience whether you will accept interruptions (questions, comments) during your presentation or prefer them at the end. Tell them at the start if you have a handout (give it at the end) and if they should take notes.
- Keep your jokes to a minimum – it's easy to offend someone in your audience. But do SMILE!
- Use the screen only for key words, pictures, lists, numbers. Keep your slides or overheads simple: one idea per slide, maximum four lines, maximum seven words per line. Use big type: letters should be 5mm high on the screen for every metre from the back of the room.
- Use A5 cards or A4 sheets for your notes, not the screen. Number these cards/sheets in case you drop them. If you don't know what to do with your hands, hold your notes in front of you (but not at chest level: lower, then raise them to read them).
- Speak clearly. Make continuous eye contact all round. Let everyone in the room feel that you are personally addressing him or her. But don't stare.
- Don't hide behind the lectern. Let everyone see you in the open.
- Rehearse, rehearse, rehearse your presentation. If a presentation is under-rehearsed, the audience suffers. Hesitation, back-tracking, lack of order, and omission or excessive repetition of key points are some of the faults that get low marks and hamper understanding.
- Questions: repeat every question from the audience. This lets everyone hear the question, and makes sure that you have understood it. Be patient with "silly" questions. Limit questions to two per person. Don't hesitate to say, "I don't know" – and then invite an answer from the audience.
- Finish when everything is going well ("Leave the audience crying for more" is a good showbiz maxim). End on or before time. Don't thank the audience for listening to you (did they have a choice?)

Some parts of this set of guidelines come from the stage. A presenter can adopt many theatrical techniques to help him communicate to an audience (gesturing, voice projection, whispering to achieve attention, pregnant pauses are some of them). No harm is done if he thinks of himself as a showman, utilising the techniques of stagecraft to support his arguments.

Finally, let's look at Winston Churchill's "The Scaffolding of Rhetoric", in which he wrote of the four principles of effective oral communication:

1. correctness of diction and short words.
2. rhythm, like blank verse.
3. accumulation of argument; a series of facts all pointing in a common direction.
4. analogy "appeals to everyday knowledge of the hearer and invites him to decide problems...by the standard of the nursery and the heart."

Meetings

Some of the most valuable communications take place in meetings, where the leader can make his presence felt, and where he can take advantage of the opportunity to listen and watch. Since it is frequently the leader who convenes the meeting, he must take steps to ensure its productive effectiveness.

Firstly, though, there's a lot to be said for not calling a meeting at all, but using instead the many other means of communication – phone, memo, e-mail, and simple face-to-face discussion – to resolve a problem or to present information. Secondly, it is a sound plan to challenge some of the traditions surrounding meetings. For example, many highly productive meetings have been held in rooms with no chairs. Others, expected to last an hour, have been convened an hour before lunchtime.

If you decide that calling a meeting is the best way to get something done, take account of the following sequence of events:

Sharpen your behaviour when Convening a Meeting

When preparing the meeting, be sure about:

- its purpose and expected outcome
- the process to be used: presentation, problem-solving, workshop, etc. or it may be for exchange of facts, views, diary dates (for a standing committee whose members have little other contact) or exchange of work/job status and problems/solutions (for a business group review meeting)
- when and where it will be held
- how long it will take (and stick to this!)
- who should be present: who can contribute usefully to the discussion
- who should not be present

A few days before the meeting:

- distribute a detailed agenda, listing the first five of the above plus the names of those who will speak (if formally). Tough items first
- include supporting documents for some items. Don't wait to distribute them at the meeting
- state the format of each item on the agenda – presentation for information-giving, round-table discussion for agreement and ownership, problem-solving (using Creative Problem Solving tools) for an action plan, small workshop groups for active participation
- check that the agenda has been received and understood
- make sure the room is ready; table(s), seats, flipcharts, projector(s), handouts

Then, on the day:

- be there first
- start the meeting on time, even if not every invited person is there. Start with a grabber, a motivator or a statement of benefits – or just the agenda. Restate the purpose of the meeting.
- stick to the agenda. Digressions are relegated to "Any other business" (if this is on the agenda) or deferred to another meeting or ignored.
- make sure that someone takes notes (minutes), especially recording all decisions for action
- manage the discussion. Let everyone have his or her say; encourage the diffident, dissuade the loudmouths. Keep everyone on the subject. Ask for explanations.
- summarise from time to time
- cut discussion short if it gets heated, or if no decision seems to be coming (be very firm!)
- defuse conflict by calling on everyone in the room to resolve it. If necessary, call a halt and re-convene the meeting 24 hours later.
- get agreement on a 'path forward' – an action plan (who does what by when) and date and place of the next meeting
- end on time, even if it means deferring a subject to a later date.

Afterwards:

- distribute the minutes or action notes, as soon as possible, to all participants and everyone affected by the outcome of the meeting.

> Never call a meeting without announcing the expected outcome, and
> never hold a meeting without an outcome. *(Lorraine Monroe)*

What others have written
Meredith Belbin looked at the performance of "teams" (mostly
short-term, project-related task groups). He identified eight team
roles which we can easily re-cast as meeting roles. The first two are
unquestionably leaders:
The Co-ordinator (originally "The Chairman") who pulls together
and focuses the team's efforts.
The Shaper, the driver within the group.
Other roles include The Plant, The Monitor Evaluator, The
Company Worker, The Team Worker, The Resource Investigator
and The Complete Finisher. Belbin later added The Specialist.

Listening

Hearing and understanding what other people have to say is just as vital for
effective communication as speaking and writing. The speaker makes an effort to
communicate his thoughts, so the listener should make an equal effort to hear and
understand them.

A leader asks the right questions. He asks questions which he knows the other(s) can
answer and to which he, the leader, wants to know the answer. He asks simple, direct
questions. He asks 'open' questions that require more than "Yes" and "No" answers.

A leader listens at meetings, in briefings, in group gatherings. He lets others speak,
give their views and opinions and get things off their chest. The leader doesn't
interrupt, but patiently waits to hear what the others have to say. He asks questions,
waits patiently for the answers and learns. ("You aren't learning much when your
mouth is moving.")

> List, list, O list! *Hamlet*

The leader puts effort into listening. He listens as though he has subsequently to
report the conversation to a third party. He makes notes if it's appropriate to do so
(he may ask permission first), and he takes time afterwards to digest what he has
heard.

The effective leader asks the speaker to repeat sentences, either without change or paraphrased, if he thinks that he has not understood the speaker, or has misunderstood him. He repeats key phrases aloud, to ensure that what the speaker said is what he meant. He paraphrases the speaker's arguments and voices his interpretation of them, to ensure his understanding of them.

As a result of listening well, the leader strengthens his position. He is perceived as a trusting and trustworthy person, and he earns respect for his empathy with others. The net effect of attending carefully to what others have to say is to create an impression of authority and support combined with wisdom, of courtesy and urbanity. These traits go well with leadership.

Sharpen your behaviour as a Listener

- Listen hard. You may have to report the speaker's arguments to someone else.
- Ask the right questions.
- Make notes (ask permission).
- Don't interrupt, even a silence. Wait for the speaker to finish, and wait for answers to your questions.
- Clarify key points. Ask for explanation. Paraphrase or repeat aloud the speaker's propositions.

6. Mister Trustful

If he doesn't trust his followers, a leader is not a leader. Trust needs courage; it's difficult, precarious and reciprocal. Trust boosts morale, cuts down the need for supervision and encourages initiative.

Trust is one of the cornerstones of leadership, a characteristic without which leadership cannot exist. It is a key ingredient in separating the role of leader from the function of manager.

A manager who has no confidence in the members of the group he manages is no leader. Trusting them means having the courage to give people the opportunity to

- make decisions (and mistakes)
- prove and develop themselves
- create their own environment and ways of working.

If trust does not exist, suspicion will replace it, and an atmosphere of ill-feeling, rancour and non-co-operation can invade the workplace. Leadership, in such circumstances, can only be assertive and autocratic all the time, which is not conducive to effectiveness.

Trust must be reciprocal to work. The leader must be trustworthy; group members must demonstrate their trust in him (more about Trustworthiness later). Trust is precarious – once broken, it is virtually impossible to reinstate. Trust is risky – it can bring failure as well as success. And trust is hard to give – it's easier to be mistrustful, to view everyone as a possible source of ineptitude, failure and delay.

> I have often found that a man who trusts nobody is apt to be the kind of man whom nobody trusts. *(Harold Macmillan)*

On the positive side, trust boosts morale. People who know that the leader trusts them will perform up to the limit of their capabilities. They will, if their personalities allow, consult with the leader in times of doubt and dilemma, thus demonstrating their acceptance of the trust given to them. This can also take the form of upwards delegation, in which a group member delegates to the leader all or part of a task, for reasons of workload or competence.

Trust allows a group member to challenge the leader's vision, or his manager's commands, within the bounds that trust imposes. Mutual trust allows conflicts to be resolved by seeking the cause, rather than blame and recrimination. Disagreement and misunderstanding are more easily reconciled where trust exists.

On the negative side, trust can be misplaced, and lead to failure. The leader may over-estimate the competence of a group or its individual members, assigning them a task which they cannot perform. Or a group member may abuse the trust placed in him, with dire consequences. An example is the behaviour of Judas Iscariot; Jesus trusted him to act honourably and he failed.

And trust may be unjustified: the group leader must challenge the motives and actions of a group member who, although apparently willing and competent, nevertheless may give the impression of running his own agenda – of having himself or some other cause to fight for. A degree of suspicion is warranted.

> Who naught suspects is easily deceived. *(Petrarch)*

Trust, developed and accepted, has many ramifications in its application. It cuts down on the need for supervision, and gives individuals responsibility through delegation and empowerment. People who are trusted enjoy work which is wider-ranging and more challenging.

Trust increases the opportunities for initiative and imagination. Challenge is encouraged and accepted. Decision-making can be delegated if trust exists, with increasing responsibility and authority. Risk can be delegated too, allowing a group member to make his own assessment of the degree of risk involved in a plan or an action, and to decide whether to share his view with the leader and the group, and whether to continue or abandon.

Trust allows an individual to become (and be recognised as) an expert in a specialist field. When the leader sees a need for a specific expertise within the group, he assigns an individual, or invites volunteers. The selected group member can be trained and can shift his activities into a new area of expertise, to become a trusted contributor to the aims of the group.

Sharpen your behaviour as 'Mister Trustful'

- Trust the individuals around you to the maximum, until you know where the limits are. Then institute controls.

- Remember that people are motivated to do their best for the group (unless they have been demotivated by design or by negligence). Allow them to do their best, and learn what their best consists of. And remember that a satisfied need ceases to motivate.
- Tolerate others' mistakes in decision-making, in performance, in risk-taking. Help them to learn from these mistakes (and share the learning with the whole group). Initiate a formal 'lessons learned' process.
- Invite consultation and feedback. Ease off the controls, check on performance as infrequently as possible.

7. The Delegator

The loneliness of leadership is eased through trust and through delegation, done properly and well. Successful sharing of tasks and projects includes evaluation of the situation and of the delegate(s), handing over authority with responsibility (but not accountability), self-control on the part of the leader, monitoring the process and learning from failure.

The mad rush to improve performance and pursue excellence has multiplied the number of demands on executives and managers. These demands come from every part of business and personal life, and they increasingly seem incompatible and impossible:

•   Think strategically and invest in the future – but keep the numbers up today.

•   Be entrepreneurial and take risks – but don't cost the business anything by failing.

•   Continue to do everything you're currently doing even better – and spend more time communicating with employees, serving on teams, and launching new projects.

•   Know every detail of your business – but delegate more responsibility to others.

•   Become passionately dedicated to 'visions' and fanatically committed to carrying them out – but be flexible, responsive and able to change direction quickly.

•   Speak up, be a leader, set the direction – but be participative, listen well, co-operate.

•   Throw yourself wholeheartedly into the entrepreneurial game and the long hours it takes – and stay fit.

•   Succeed, succeed, succeed – and raise terrific children. *(Rosbeth Moss Kanter)*

I could add a few more paradoxes to this list, but I'll content myself with one:

"Commit yourself to the aims of those who appointed you in their own image, and never forget who's paying your salary – but show that you can breathe new life into the business, bring new ideas to the party and raise standards of performance all round."

These paradoxes point up the loneliness – and the breadth – of the manager-as-leader's role. He is on his own, juggling the demands of his position as manager of a work group with those of the people to whom he reports, his bosses. It is in this situation that his leadership behaviour is tried and tested. An effective manager recognises the isolation of his position, his inability to share many of his concerns, his heavy workload, the demands on his time. In today's business and voluntary organisations, the manager is expected to delegate: as leader, his load can be lessened by sharing or delegating tasks.

The effective solution to some of the paradoxes we have listed, and the tensions they create, lies in the emotional content of a leader's characteristics. The manager-as-leader knows whom to trust and how to trust. He knows where to assign his priorities, and how to deal with the conflicts arising from the incompatibility of the demands on him, first as a manager and second as a leader. He delegates tasks and projects (and the responsibility for achievement), not from the front, nor from behind, but from the middle, as a member of the group, a colleague and co-worker.

Although a leader may sometimes have to impose himself upon his group in an assertive manner, many situations call for the sharing of tasks. The process of sharing starts with communication and culminates in delegation. Delegation increases the leader's time and capacity for the tasks that he alone must perform. At the same time it gives others the opportunity of developing and proving themselves, as part of the process of developing a successor. Delegation helps others to grow. It identifies future leaders.

Delegation and empowerment are two of the ways in which the leader demonstrates trust in group members. Empowerment is part of the managerial toolkit; the manager can assign to his subordinates the freedom and power to make their own decisions (that is, by extending the boundaries of their authority and responsibility) and to take action without reference to him.

Delegation means entrusting one or more members of the group with a specific task or project. It may be done without consulting, or without the knowledge of, other members of the group or the people to whom the leader is accountable. Or it may be initiated, discussed and even monitored publicly.

Delegation can start with the simplest of assignments: a group member may bring a problem to the leader, who asks him to propose a solution. The leader may challenge the solution (within the bounds of trust), but if he thinks that it is an acceptable solution, he tells the proposer to get on with it. He demonstrates trust by opening doors, smoothing paths and providing appropriate resources for the delegate.

When a task is delegated, the process usually includes the delegation of authority. But it has been said that the only reason for delegating authority is to retain control. The leader must decide if control (a manager's province) is really what he wants. If he accepts that control is unnecessary, or can be minimal, authority need not be formally vested in the delegate. This offers an excellent opportunity for the delegate to develop and demonstrate his own leadership behaviour. But, whether or not authority is vested in the delegate, the leader is accountable for the result of the delegated task, and he must be prepared to defend the actions of the delegate and his own decisions.

Upwards or reverse delegation is a valuable process in a group which is well-knit, well loaded with work, and in which trust is prevalent. Group members invite the leader to handle tasks and projects which, for reasons of competence or overload, they are unable or unwilling to handle themselves. This process strengthens the link between the group and its leader, allowing the leader to gain a further measure of understanding of the individuals in the group.

Delegating isn't easy

Delegation doesn't come easily to many people, who argue (to themselves) that "It takes as long to explain the job as for me to do it" or "If I want something done properly (*that is, in my way*) I have to do it myself." Delegation means accepting that how someone else carries out the task may differ from the delegator's way. The effective leader has learnt to let go, to view delegation as a necessary and useful part of his role as leader. He has learnt to be tolerant of mistakes, and to accept the risk of failure.

The leader must be sure in his own mind that he is not delegating a task which he doesn't want to do himself, unless it's for reasons of workload or competence. He could and should delegate a task that he would like to perform himself. The leader may have to force himself to delegate. And he is able to delegate in bad times as well as when things are going well.

The leader avoids excessive delegation, which is an indicator of abdication of the leadership (and the management) role. If too many tasks or projects, which properly are the responsibility of the manager-as-leader, are delegated, group members seize and retain the authority which has been given to them, and with it the power and eventually the leadership role.

Delegation may be short-term, for one project or for a fixed period of time (for example, during a colleague's absence). In this case, the delegate may have little pride in achievement. Or it may be long-term, with occasional appraisal and evaluation of the delegate's performance and the accomplishment of the task. Either way, the leader's role in the process is supportive but not obvious, watchful but not oppressive, helpful but not magisterial.

Delegation requires, on the part of the leader, self-discipline – that is, holding back from watching every move and monitoring every aspect of the performance of the person to whom the task has been delegated. He avoids seizing the reins when crisis threatens. If he does take over ("Let me handle this") he risks losing the trust and confidence of all the members of his group, and breeding an atmosphere of non-co-operation and demotivation. But he is allowed to ask the delegate, "What would you like me to do?"

Another necessary characteristic in the leader is patience. Delegating a task involves time and effort

- in explanation
- in asking for feedback from the delegate to ensure understanding
- in confirming (or asking the delegate to confirm) the details in writing; the deadlines, the resources (people, equipment, funds), the boundaries of assigned authority, the reporting and consultation expected
- in repeating the objectives from time to time
- in coaching
- in supporting
- in frequently monitoring and discussing progress and results
- in giving feedback.

Delegation requires care and effort, on both sides. It can fail, or be ineffective, or take more time and effort than predicted, or create ill-will. These are some of the risks in delegation. The benefits, however, far outweigh them, and delegation is a course of action that is a significant component of effective leadership.

What happens if trust is misplaced, if the delegate fails, or abuses his authority? If the leader trusts a group member too far, or assigns a task beyond the delegate's competence? The monitoring process must be designed to meet such contingencies without restricting the delegate's performance. To ensure timely warning of a shortfall, the leader discusses progress with the delegate and talks with others who interface with him; he watches the delegate perform and studies the results, having established agreement in advance that these devices will be used. If, in the end, the project fails through inappropriate choice of delegate, the leader admits his mistake, learns from it, and revises his assessment of the delegate.

Preparing to Delegate

While delegation cannot be a wholly hands-off process, the degree to which the leader needs to know every step taken by his delegate, to be kept informed of every decision, action and (let's face it) mistake, requires fine judgement – another characteristic of a good leader. This judgement will be based on three factors in the most important aspect of delegation – the thorough preparation of the delegated task:

1. An assessment of the competence, the workload, the interests and the aspirations of the delegate. The leader must be confident in the delegate's capability of handling the task: does he have the necessary skills, time, energy? Does he really want to do it? (He may need to be persuaded.) Can he be trusted?

2. The situation in which the process is taking place: is the task or project part of a larger plan, whose success depends on the outcome of the delegated task? Is it appropriate – for example, a task which will stretch the delegate's capabilities and strengths, or expose his weaknesses? Should the leader handle it? What is the expected outcome? Where are the boundaries of authority, the limits of delegated power? Are the resources and the time span adequate?

3. The people with whom the delegate is expected to work: do they understand all the details of the delegated task? Do they know how their own tasks and authority relate to those of the delegate? Will they accept the delegate's authority?

Finally, the leader and the delegate discuss concerns on both sides:

*   they talk about possible alternative outcomes, including failure.

- together they consider possible obstacles to success.
- they agree on the ways in which consultation and monitoring during the project can best be handled.

A written document describing the task, the responsibilities and authority, the expected outcome, the resources, and listing the agreed concerns and their resolution can eliminate subsequent conflict.

What others have written

Kenneth Blanchard identifies four leadership styles which can be applied to the process of delegation:

1. a directive approach, for work on a short time-scale or for new employees

2. a coaching approach, in which the task and the method of accomplishing it are given by the leader

3. a supporting style, often used between peers, with trust accompanied by offers of help and support

4. a delegating approach, which involves low direction and low support, presupposing that the delegate is highly competent and that the leader has considerable trust in him.

Sharpen your behaviour as a Delegator

- Do nothing on your own that can be shared.
- Know the delegate. Understand his unique situation, his ambitions and motivations, before starting the process. Build a relationship. Trust, trustworthiness, understanding are the keys. Soften up possible resistance with compliments.
- Don't just delegate tasks, delegate projects. Entrust the delegate with the planning, so that he knows the background, the reasons, the broader picture of the project. Offer projects that you would like to handle, not those that you don't like. Don't dump.
- Discuss concerns; possible alternative outcomes, including failure; obstacles to success; consultation and monitoring during the project.
- Give as much authority to the delegate as you can. Stand by your decision in case of conflict or failure.
- Give support. Smooth the delegate's path by providing resources and encouragement.
- Treat delegation as a stepping-stone to eventual leadership. Delegate, with minimal supervision, to your chosen successor.

- Give credit for success. Share responsibility for failure.

It's a good idea to start delegating by empowering a group. If you do, the list above applies, plus:

- If the group is to have its own leader, help in the selection of the leader. Influence the group's choice in favour of a person whom you have identified as a likely leader. Voice your own proposal, lobby on his behalf, provide opportunities for your preferred leader to demonstrate his skills.
- The empowered group needs direction (goals, measurements), knowledge (useful, practical, applicable), skills, resources (people, money, time, materials) and support (approval, encouragement, path-smoothing). The manager-as-leader can provide all of these except the skills (training may be called for).
- Encourage the group to determine its own task priorities, task-handling and task-fulfilment by setting broadly-based ('bottom line') goals. Check and monitor visibly and thoroughly, but as infrequently as possible.
- Invite consultation and feedback. Keep an open door, walk the talk, refresh motivation by communicating (views from the outside, news of the big organisation, plans and activities that can affect the group and its goals).
- Empower group members to be the ones to say "Yes" to outsiders, not just "No."

The four steps in delegating

1. Prepare thoroughly to delegate. Plan all the parameters – task, expected outcome, resources, responsibilities, limits of authority, timing, expected feedback.
2. Brief thoroughly: first face-to-face, then with written confirmation. Check for understanding and concerns.
3. During the assignment, be available for consultation and help. Be supportive. Remove obstacles, offer training, defend the delegate(s). Check and control as little as possible.
4. On completion of the assignment, invite comment, face-to-face and in writing, on the task and its outcome, on the learning from the exercise, on future delegation of projects.

8. The Rock

Steady as a Rock, the leader demonstrates dependability, trustworthiness and integrity, as well as proof of competence, high principles and strong convictions. He under-promises and over-delivers, doesn't shrink from expressing doubt, and takes time to think.

The Rock exudes honesty and sincerity, as well as trustworthiness and sound moral principle. Consistently demonstrated probity contributes to the perception of a trustworthy leader. He is a Rock that group members can depend on, reliable, dependable, upright.

An effective leader demonstrates integrity in everything he does. He is open and honest with the members of his group, and with everyone he comes into contact with. Insinuation, inference and double-dealing are not part of his stock-in-trade. He can respect confidences – he can remain silent when necessary – he may bite his tongue when he thinks fit – but his words always reflect his real thoughts, and his actions are always founded on strongly-held convictions. Such upright behaviour does not come naturally. It requires constant effort to start with, and self-discipline to sustain it.

Of course people, including leaders, are not perfect, and human foibles and failings enter into the equation. The aspiring leader as well as the incumbent leader understand this, and make allowances for their own imperfections, and for the imperfections of others. The leader carefully develops a style of behaviour that allows him to take time to think before acting and speaking, and to admit his mistakes. It's not easy, and can be frustrating and painful, but its results are visible and satisfying.

The effective leader has high moral principles. He does not lie, cheat or steal. He is pure in thought, word and deed. Well, almost. He tries hard to observe the Ten Commandments, the Eightfold Path, the Shari'a and other codes of behaviour. But there are times when being perfect is not the best way to get things done. The leader knows that the whole truth may hurt or at least create disbelief. That nothing but the truth may lead to misunderstanding. That exaggeration and over-optimism may help to convince his listeners. That the straight and narrow path may not lead where the group should go. But – a big BUT – he does not use these deceits for his own benefit. His strongly-held convictions allow him flexibility in helping the group to meet its objectives, and he is prepared to answer to the group or anyone else for his decisions to use it. He is open about his actions, and may decide to share his decisions, and his reasons for them, with his group. Secrecy is not a working tool.

> It is a mistake to shrink from stating the true facts to the [group]. *(Winston Churchill)* [So give it to 'em straight, bad news as well as good. But give them the good news first, and make the bad news sound like a challenge for the group to meet.]

Being Trustworthy

Trustworthiness can be developed by the leader, and demonstrated when the occasion arises. Group members, and others, come to recognise and appreciate rock-like steadfastness, and even take advantage of it by using the leader (the Rock) as a confessor or an intellectual prop on the basis, not of friendliness, but of respect. They appreciate the leader's contribution to their work and their personal lives, and they raise the status of the leader, in their eyes, to that of a reliable, solid foundation for the group's activities.

Like trust, trustworthiness is one of the principal burdens of leadership. When trust is key to command, trust is all there is, and no other relationship can take its place. Members of the group rely on trust alone to follow the leader, irrespective of the strength of other arguments and substantiated reasons. Blind trust is the essence of soldiering; every military man and woman is trained to obey, instantly and without reflection, orders from above, and to trust implicitly in their feasibility. The trustworthiness and presumed infallibility of those giving the orders is not questioned when immediate action is demanded.

In this age of better education and claims to the rights of the individual, trust is being replaced by cynicism, and trustworthiness by power. This doesn't, however, deny the premise that trustworthiness is a vital component of leadership; it's just that this characteristic must now be visibly demonstrated, even promoted, to ensure that the leader can function with minimal power – which, in any case, he may not have. Demonstration of trustworthiness includes proof of competence; however honest and upright a manager is, he is not considered trustworthy, and therefore is not a leader, if he is incompetent in his profession as manager. After all, you wouldn't trust an honest, upright dentist if he wasn't competent, would you?

Trustworthiness can be developed. Keeping secrets, respecting confidences and offering objective advice are relatively easy, though they require discipline and, for some people, a drastic change in the ways in which they relate to others. What is more difficult is the communication of one's thoughts, ideas and plans – one's visions – as part of the process of leading a group. Under the heading of Communicating, we refer to openness and clarity: these characteristics are allied to trustworthiness, but only insofar as the leader is right, or seen to be right. Successful soothsayers and sages of old kept their positions of power by making sure that their predictions were either right (for example, by *really* knowing when the next eclipse was due) or capable of being interpreted as right, through ambiguous phrasing.

I cannot recommend ambiguous phrasing as a means of demonstrating trustworthiness, but care in the communication of plans and ideas pays off. If the leader has doubts about the feasibility of his plan of action, he expresses these doubts, and lets the group make its own judgements and suggest improvements. If he doesn't have enough data to be sure of the direction in which to head, he invites the group to help him gather more data before finalising the details of his plan. To the group's questions he may answer, "I don't know" and thereby enhance his trustworthiness. The leader doesn't fudge.

> When in doubt, tell the truth. *(Mark Twain)*

> If you tell the truth, you don't have to remember anything. *(Anon)*

Promises

Keeping promises is an obligation of effective leadership. Breaking a promise has an immediate and disastrous effect on morale, which takes a long time to recover. Breaking a promise made to even one group member will weaken the fabric of the group; word gets around. Maybe it's best never to make a promise, or to hedge it about with provisos and qualifications and ambiguity so that there is a fallback position if the promise can't be kept. But this is fudging, and won't work more than once. The trustworthy leader always makes commitments which are well thought out, which require equal commitment from the group, and which are recognised from the outset as practicable even if the task is herculean. He doesn't over-promise and under-deliver. He doesn't allow others to do this. He is rock-steady.

> A leader's calculations about a particular decision may be wrong, but the trustworthiness of a leader's character offers a sufficient counterweight on the balance sheet. *(Stephen F. Hayward)* [And, through trustworthiness,

leaders provide reassurance and confidence.]

Sharpen your behaviour as a Rock

- Know the principles you live by, and stick to them. Don't prevaricate, or hedge, or sit on the fence.
- Practise honesty. Don't lie, cheat or steal (but do by all means copy the good ideas of others!).
- Keep your promises. Under-promise and over-deliver.
- Drive out fear. Eliminate punishment. Use the carrot, not the stick
- Invite others to share their personal issues with you.
- Keep secrets, respect confidences.
- Be open in your communications, clear and unambiguous – bad news as well as good.
- Take time to think things through.
- Admit your mistakes.

9. The Hero

With increasing competition from popular heroes, the leader puts effort into visible exemplary behaviour. He accepts his responsibility to be looked up to, to be emulated.

The role model is an increasingly difficult position to fill. The Economist, writing about fame in 1997, concluded that "As people have become more cynical, better informed and more egalitarian, so politicians, soldiers and saints have lost their attraction as heroes that once satisfied popular demand." Today's heroes are those who appeal to the emotions; television celebrities and pop stars, footballers and other sportsmen, and any individual selected by vox populi or the media as worthy of attention. But some leaders are still regarded with awe and deference by members of the groups they lead.

Whether as teacher, parent, manager, politician, voluntary group leader or sports team captain, many leaders are perceived as hero and role model by and for their followers. Children at home and at school identify their parents and teachers as role models, although increasingly sports and entertainment personalities are usurping this position. Politicians are seen – or rather, see themselves – as role models, while some parts of society have adopted religious leaders as their role models. In business situations, managers become role models for those who seek to be promoted in their place.

Role modelling doesn't come easily or naturally, and many people in leadership positions ignore this responsibility to their followers. We have all seen many so-called leaders who fall short of the standards expected of heroes. Politicians notoriously equivocate and bluff. Parents are no better (and mostly no worse) than average in terms of morals and principles. Teachers, while conscious of their modelling roles, cannot act the part to the exclusion of normal human foibles. Sports and entertainment personalities are often corrupted by their popularity and the very adulation that created it.

> The Hero can be Poet, Prophet, King, Priest or what you will, according to the kind of world he finds himself born into. *(Thomas Carlyle)*

What should a leader aim for, as a hero? It's easy to preach an ideal such as humility, but it's also unrealistic to expect a leader to behave as though he were a divine being. The best we can hope for is a consciousness of being looked up to, a realisation that one is fallible, and behaviour according to the principle that one makes mistakes. A goal for the leader to aspire to is excellence in four fundamental traits of leadership: vision, trust, integrity and self-knowledge.

A leader acknowledges his mistakes openly. He invites (positive) criticism. He thinks before he acts, to minimise the need for post-action damage control. He trusts, delegates and shares. In short, he tries a bit harder to be an effective member of the group, a *primus inter pares*, accepting responsibility for the group's actions and providing an example, a paradigm, for others to follow. He does not want to be a tin god, insubstantial and weak, with nothing but show for others to emulate.

> Leadership is practised not so much in words as in attitude and in actions. *(Harold Geneen, former chairman of ITT Corporation)*

The leader's behaviour reflects his convictions and principles. He believes in continuous learning, so he (visibly) improves himself by listening to experts, taking training courses, and reading relevant books. He believes in high-quality communication, so he spends time and effort on preparing for meetings, for face-to-face discussions, for telephone calls and video conferences. He takes trouble with his letters, faxes and e-mails.

The leader is convinced of the value of developing people, so he offers opportunities for formal training. He coaches and mentors his colleagues. He discusses their weaknesses and mistakes immediately and positively. His integrity is a by-word in the group. He challenges his colleagues' ideas positively – not "Why?" but "Why not?" In short, he works hard at his leadership behaviour and encourages others to behave in the same way.

As hero, the leader accepts the additional responsibility of representing the group to the outside world. He is the ambassador, the spokesman for the group when needed. He is the channel of communication for messages to and from the group. These roles are accepted by the group, even encouraged and applauded. Others outside the group know that the group is approachable through the leader.

The leader will change with time, due to

- added experience
- change in his expectations and in others' expectations of him

- increased skills
- increase in age relative to (new) colleagues in the group.

As a result of these personal changes, the leader's position as role model changes. He is viewed more as a source of wisdom and experience, less as an inspiration and driving force. Group members will respect him more for what he knows than for what he does. A new hero will take his place when group members need or want to be refreshed, re-motivated and revitalised. Le roi est mort, vive le roi! (More on this in "The Future of Leadership in Management" on page 112.)

> Every hero becomes a bore at last. *(Ralph Waldo Emerson)*

Sharpen your behaviour as a Hero

- Think of the people you have regarded as leaders, good and bad. What were the characteristics of their behaviour? How did they influence their followers, orally and non-verbally?
- Leadership can be communicated and taught by example. And example is contagious.
- Work hard at your leadership behaviour until it becomes unconscious and habitual. Accept self-discipline as an example to others.
- Act and demonstrate consistency.
- Show pride in what you are and what you do. Look confident, even if you don't feel it.
- Accept that others see you as you are, with your strengths and weaknesses, your successes and failures. Show humility in yourself and respect for others.
- Modelling the role of leader is a responsibility, but need not be a burden. Accept it, live up to it, and don't regret it when it passes.

10. The Self-Manager

Self-confidence combined with humility enhances the leader's managerial competence. He knows and exploits his strengths, corrects his weaknesses, exercises self-control and uses self-doubt to challenge his own behaviour.

Successful leaders often indulge in self-delusion, believing themselves to be more effective, more popular or more virtuous than is justified. In the next few paragraphs, such a leader can learn how to understand and manage his own thoughts, feelings and behaviour – as always, for the benefit of the group he leads.

The leader knows his own strengths – call this self-confidence – and exploits them for the benefit of the group. For example, if he is an exceptional communicator, he uses this talent to ensure the group's understanding of his vision, and gain the commitment of every member of the group to it. If he is confident in his role-modelling skills, he parades them in front of the group, to give group members confidence in their hero and to help them see themselves as future leaders. His managerial strengths are exploited in the same way. For instance, if his organisational skills are above average, he puts effort into organising the group and its activities in the most effective way, whether this means stability, flexibility or simply re-structuring.

The leader is aware of his own weaknesses too. He practises modesty, even humility, and doesn't let his limitations hamper his leadership style and behaviour. He manages his affairs so that he avoids decisions and actions where he knows that he performs less well. For example, if he is not confident in his judgement of risk, the leader involves the whole group in the decision-making process. If he knows that he is not a good delegator, he invites group members to propose ways in which they can contribute to the managerial functions within the group – though he takes care to judge every such proposal on its value to the group, and on its likely outcome. He also takes steps to correct his weaknesses, to improve himself by continuous self-learning, by practice, by inviting feedback (it may be painful) and by inviting coaching and mentoring – provided that his weaknesses are behavioural and not personality-based.

> The greatest of faults, I should say, is to be conscious of none. *(Thomas Carlyle)*

But a weakness may be turned to advantage. For example, a leader may demonstrate the (personality) weakness of slow-wittedness – he may be considered by others as hesitant and dull. But the flip-side of this characteristic may be thoroughness, an ability to think things through and come to a conclusion that takes all the relevant factors into account. This is unquestionably a characteristic of an effective leader. Or his stress level may be evident in his verbal outbursts, or in bursts of frenetic activity. He can control this stress through exercise and mind-calming strategies, but he must first recognise that stress can generate useful physical and creative energy. It is important, therefore, that the leader knows himself well, understands his strengths and weaknesses, and recognises how they may best be used to the advantage of the group. He knows that, as leader, he is also the servant of the group. All his energy goes into serving the purposes and aims of the group of which he is part.

> Leadership begins with learning to know and control oneself; then, and only then, can one lead, enable and control others. *(The Leadership Trust)*

The leader knows how to manage stress in himself and in others. He re-directs and exploits its energy in order to relieve its damaging effects. He allows time for relaxation and sleep. His self-discipline tends to be spartan, while his self-denial releases energy for the important roles of leading.

Self-assessment does not mean self-deception. While self-confidence and optimism are vital and may include an exaggerated view of one's capabilities, deceiving oneself and others about one's competences can have disastrous consequences for the individual and the group. And self-confidence translated into self-love excludes solicitude for others, as well as an introversion which isolates the individual from any group.

Self-confidence, easily perceived as – or transformed into – arrogance, has a useful counterpart in self-doubt, which is the internalised form of the challenging process, itself an important part of leadership as a whole. Momentary self-doubt allows the leader-as-visionary and as communicator to question what he is doing. He can stand apart from himself and use his imagination to foretell the effects of his behaviour on the group, and to change it if necessary. He blames no one but himself for his shortcomings. He accepts responsibility for all he does.

Self-restraint is a rare virtue, requiring enviable self-discipline and objective understanding of one's momentary relationship with others. A leader who knows when to be discreet and stay in the background does this because he knows that his intervention can lead to an undesirable outcome. An effective leader knows when to hold back, to master (even hide) his emotions, to deny himself the pleasure of participation. He doesn't have to do this all the time – this would mean being untrue to himself – but he knows when the time is right to step into the shadows, to let someone else (a potential successor?) take up the challenge.

And the self-conscious leader knows when (and how, and for how long) to hand over the mantle of leadership, to relinquish the role, the power and the responsibility, and to delegate them to someone better able to carry the burden of the situation.

Self-development

> Leadership and learning are indispensable to each other. *(John F. Kennedy)*

The leader practises continuous self-development or 'renewal.' He watches and reads in order to learn. He reflects on his performance from time to time. He knows what information can add to his professional knowledge and creativity, and rejects the irrelevant. He knows how to turn knowledge into wisdom. He values professional self-development above loyalty. He plans his career path for at least the next five years, and tells his bosses that he seeks leadership roles. He creates and seizes opportunities to progress along that path, a course which may conflict with the goals of the larger organisation. He sticks to his objective, and turns down opportunities which conflict with it. His allegiance to the larger organisation is secondary to his personal goals. And he knows that his leadership skills will develop and grow in spite of the organisation, rather than because of it.

That leadership behaviour, while inherent, is not instinctive in some people has given rise to a raft of symposia, courses and training programmes to help managers and others learn and develop leadership talents, under such titles as "organisational behaviour". They are seldom as productive as everyday experience, although off-the-job training brings benefits such as time to re-think one's effectiveness as leader, to provide opportunities for delegation and to learn how others behave as leaders. A manager who is ambitious for the complementary leadership role recognises that experience, rather than schoolroom learning in a non-threatening environment, is the key to success.

> The only real training for leadership is leadership. *(Anthony Jay)*

The leader-in-waiting can take personal development into his own hands, by putting effort into developing each leadership behaviour, by following the advice in this book, and seizing on-the-job opportunities as they arise to practise each skill.

> Successful leaders have the core competence of accurate self-assessment – they know their own strengths and weaknesses. As a result, they are better able to assess strengths and weaknesses in others, and to determine how their strengths and weaknesses line up with certain situations. *(Steve Zeisler)*

What others have written

John Adair offers the advice that, if you do the right things, you will become a leader – do not wait for the right attitudes to appear – actions form attitudes. **Kets de Vries** tells us that, if the leader can use self-insight as a restraining force against the seductive call of power, then he or she is likely to be successful in avoiding failure. Good leaders also know how to manage stress. They know how to wait, and do not give up easily.

Warren Bennis lists four lessons of self-knowledge:
1. you are your own best teacher
2. accept responsibility and blame no one
3. you can learn anything you want to learn
4. understanding comes from reflecting on your own experience.

Stephen Covey suggests that imagination and conscience allow one to visualise one's own untapped potential, as well as to check the morality of the goals one has envisioned. One can re-script oneself so that one's behaviour is component with one's values; future decisions can be based on these values, allowing one to stand back from the emotion of a situation and to act with integrity.

Sharpen your Self-Management behaviour
- You are your own raw material.
- Release your creative potential. Dream, invent, imagine.
- Invite and accept criticism and challenge: formally, without emotion: periodically and frequently.
- Develop yourself along the career path you have chosen.
- Take time to view your own behaviour, and its effect on others, objectively

- Encourage 360-degree feedback.
- First Rule of Three: listen, listen, listen.
- Second Rule of Three: learn, learn, learn.
- Aim to correct *every* behavioural weakness.
- Learn to manage stress.
- Study your heroes, especially those who excel where you are weak.

If you are an aspiring leader

- exploit your strengths. Eliminate your weaknesses.
- invite coaching, invite mentoring. Take courses (as manager as well as leader).
- practise your leadership behaviour at every opportunity. Concentrate on one Role, then another, until you are confident with them all.
- invite, listen to, and accept criticism and 360-degree feedback.
- accept responsibility and risk, in order to learn and gain experience. Admit your mistakes.
- acquire the skills and knowledge needed by the group, together with the boundaries and constraints, the culture and the motivation.

11. The Coach

Leaders are created in different ways, but leadership behaviour is developed through experience and practice: others can give a helping hand. The leader helps people (including his successor) to develop through his own behaviour, encouragement and formal programmes.

Developing people is a key leadership role. Coaching, training and planning personal development overlap with the managerial function. They are (or should be) a significant part of the workload of any manager in a leadership role, and may take different directions, according to the individual's needs. He may inspire and empower self-development in some group members, without playing a major role in the resulting development programme. He may catalyse an individual's ambition for self-improvement, and facilitate the search for appropriate activities. Alternatively, the leader may play a more direct part in planning and executing an individual's development programme.

> Leadership is the art of influencing others to their maximum performance to accomplish any task, objective or project. *(William A. Cohen)*

Selecting and Developing the Leader

People who have responsibility for identifying leadership potential, and with authority to appoint people to positions in which leadership behaviour is expected, can help aspiring leaders to identify themselves. They can encourage and respect challenge. They can invite visionary concepts. They can create opportunities for responsibility with authority (committees, project/task groups, discussion-leading, voluntary work) in a climate of trust, integrity, interdependence and receptivity to innovation and tolerance of mistakes. They can watch the leader grow, first as an organiser, working as a group member, then as a co-ordinator, then as a representative of the group. They watch him evolving and communicating visions and strategies, and displaying trust and trustworthiness.

Managers-as-leaders are also created in other ways. There is nepotism, in which positions of power and authority are given to friends, relatives or 'deserving' supporters. The aristocracy of an organisation may indulge in nepotism, or the 'old boy network' may be consulted for proposals to fill a vacant slot. There is the 'tournament model', in which delegation is the arena, and Darwinian survival of the most adept ensures his adoption as the leader. And there is the 'selection model' in which a committee sets out the requirements that the future leader must fulfil, identifies candidates, and picks one whose qualifications appear to meet the requirements.

None of these three processes is as sure a way of finding an effective leader as the group's own process of selecting from within the group. However, we must accept that, just as most of us cannot (yet) select or elect our own managers in the workplace, so the group may not be able to influence the choice of its own leader. Assertive (authoritarian) methods take precedence when careers and livelihoods are at stake. The selection model comes closest to the ideal.

If they are looking for new leaders, the selectors can watch the performance, under stress, of each candidate, and evaluate each individual's degree of success in fulfilling the task while under pressure. If the candidate meets the criteria for performance, but his qualifications remain in doubt, the selectors can help aspiring leaders to develop themselves, by

- offering coaching and mentoring by experienced people
- ensuring that a potential leader is exposed to a broad range of tasks and opportunities for development through trust and the delegation of authority
- offering continuous feedback in the form of constructive criticism with performance orientation (accountability and benchmarking with a focus on measurement)
- formal training in the skills required by managers
- increasing a candidate's self-confidence and authority by recognising and rewarding leadership behaviour.

Potential leaders who have no ambition in that direction, even though they show latent ability, may be similarly encouraged and developed, but less formally and at a more measured pace, with more frequent checks on performance and attitude.

Followers, too, have a part to play in the development of a leader. They can and should support him, of course, but they can also offer constructive criticism as part of 360-degree feedback. They can delegate upwards. They can share their own skills and expertise with him. They can defend him against outside criticism of his performance, provided that they are satisfied that he has done his best, and learnt from his mistakes. The group *makes* the leader.

How the leader helps others to develop

A leader gets to know the individuals who make up his group – their competences, their aspirations, their needs. He is particularly sensitive to their strengths and weaknesses. He takes time to work with them, relax with them, understand their motivations. He questions and listens, he looks and learns. He keeps notes if he doesn't trust his memory, and he keeps the notes transparent, letting each person see what he has written about him. He lets every individual add notes and comments of his own.

> ...leadership, a role whose essence is getting others to do their jobs more effectively. *(Daniel Goleman)*

In working with them, and in getting reliable information about them from others, the leader gauges how each individual measures up to his or her job description, and how he or she meets the standards established for the group. He also identifies the unused strengths and latent weaknesses of each individual, in order to evaluate his or her development potential.

The leader knows what motivates them. He appreciates that money is not an employee's first reason for working, because remuneration as an employee is taken for granted. So are holidays (vacations), sick leave, insurance, and other benefits of employment. All these 'motivations' are merely bait for employment; they become motivations only when they are reduced or absent. He knows that normally motivated people are content with their lot. They get on with their work without fuss, without complaining, and with a tenacity that demonstrates interest in the work they do. On the other hand, highly motivated people stand out because of their discontent with the status quo, their creativity and their challenging and innovative attitude. Among these highly motivated people are found future leaders.

As a highly motivated person himself, the leader can transfer this motivation to others in his group. He acts out his enthusiasm, shares his knowledge, and displays dedication to the group and its goals. If the leader fully accepts the role-model aspect of his position, members of the group will be infected with his positive attitude, and behave in the same way themselves. A leader can talk and write with enthusiasm about the group's composition, its purpose, its results, and let group members share his feelings. He uses language that inspires, enthuses and excites. He helps people to grow.

> You don't have to blow out the other fellow's light to let your own shine. *(Bernard Baruch)*

With each individual, the leader can formulate a development path, either based on talks with the person involved, or independently if he prefers to adopt the assertive approach ("I know what's best for you"). He makes sure that each person in the group is empowered to develop himself or herself, and receives continuous and appropriate coaching, training, guidance and experience, commensurate with the group's needs, with the individual's competence and aspirations, and in line with the vision that has been established for the future of the group. The leader can, at the same time, identify and develop his own successor.

Coaching is an essential ingredient in the mix of personal development. It can be given by a peer or a supervisor. It can be directive (the 'push' style) or non-directive (the 'pull' style). The two styles range from instruction and advice ("This is what you should do") through guidance and (requested) feedback, to questioning and listening. This last process, the key to the non-directive style of coaching, relies on four stages of questioning:

1. creating awareness of the individual's aspirations ("What do you want to achieve?")
2. assessment of the current situation ("What is happening now?")
3. determining the options for development towards the goal ("What could you do to move forward?")
4. choosing one of the options and committing to it ("Which of these options will you take? When?")

A future leader, identified during the process of development, can be nurtured through help with 'sharpening' his inherent skills and behaviours. He can be offered training and coaching in 'soft' skills such as

- long-term prediction and creative (strategic) planning
- management of transformational change
- risk evaluation
- speaking, writing, listening
- delegation
- time management
- stress management
- conflict management.

The leader encourages individuals to focus their energies on external forces (customers, contestants, environment). He actively discourages internal politics, competition for status, in-fighting and conflict. He encourages continuous improvement, self-development and pro-active rather than reactive thinking. He inspires challenge, creativity and innovation.

It is hard to teach adults to do things, but easier to create the conditions in which they will teach themselves. *(Sir John Harvey-Jones)*

What others have written

Kenneth Blanchard tells how he and a sports coach developed a five-step coaching plan:

- tell them what you want them to do
- show them what good performance looks like
- let them do it
- observe their performance
- praise progress or re-direct

Rupert Eales-White, on the other hand, offers his concept of the questioning coach, mixing logic, empathy and appeal to group values on a shared voyage of discovery, with full commitment to action and no risk of ridicule.

John Whitmore describes people's need to find meaning and purpose in their work, and the means of self-expression as well as the self-esteem which is generated by empowerment – which itself results from good coaching. Coaching is co-operative rather than assertive, and is an effective leadership style. It is a liberating process, using open questions to lead the 'coachee' from analysis to commitment to action.

John Burdett writes of a common vision based on, *inter alia*, the complementary dimensions of leadership and coaching.

Sharpen your behaviour as a Coach

- Monitor group members' performance. Ask for their personal views.
- Use the non-directive questioning approach to allow each 'coachee' to establish his own development programme.
- Take positive steps to continuously coach and train each individual in skills in which you know he is weak.
- Encourage self-assessment and 360-degree feedback. Help an aspiring leader to exploit his strengths and to develop where he is weak.
- Recognise exceptional skill, effort, application of both, and exceptional contribution to the group's endeavours.

- Give credit in public, admonish in private.
- Remember that the learning zone lies outside the comfort zone.
- Be a source of strength for the 'coachee'.

You maybe called upon to mentor younger or less experienced people:

Sharpen your behaviour as a Mentor

- Set an example. Be a hero to your protégé. Use your role-modelling skills.
- Challenge your protégé. Set stretch goals.
- Open doors. Fight for your protégé. Facilitate his decisions and actions.
- Protect your protégé. Tolerate mistakes as part of learning.
- Sponsor your protégé. Create opportunities for your protégé to be visible to management and others who can influence his career.
- Exploit your own successes as springboards for your protégé.

Other Leadership Attributes

In addition to the leadership behaviours described in the Eleven Roles of the Leader, the following attributes are valuable, but they are not essential for effective leadership:

- **Drive, energy and enthusiasm**: the will to push a vision into action, the conviction that it's the right thing to do, the determination to see it succeed. This easily becomes an obsession, an idée fixe, intolerant of others' views. But drive transformed into ruthlessness has its place – the leader must be prepared to make tough and unpleasant decisions.

  > The art of leadership is saying No, not Yes. It's very easy to say Yes. *(Tony Blair)*

- **The use of emotion**, especially in communicating messages. The leader is fervent and passionate when driving the group, then cool and composed when restraining and re-directing. Emotion is sometimes perceived as manipulative. It needs to be controlled and inconspicuous.

- **Group orientation**. As a group member, the leader has been a follower himself, so he knows what followers expect and value.

- **Seniority and status**: related to power and authority, to role modelling, to 'charisma' and to others' perception of him as an expert. But the leader avoids inappropriate authoritarianism and the abuse of power.

- **Acting as a self-starter**. In many disciplines, in many professions, self-starting is a key competence. Initiative is part of it, but the aspiring leader also demonstrates that he can accept the responsibility of determining his own agenda and running his own show. This is good practice for the day that he has to lead others in the same direction.

  > We still do not really know in any detail how effective leaders should behave or how they are best developed. *(Edgar H. Schein)*

- **Focus on measurement**, with benchmarks inside and outside the organisation (an essential part of managerial expertise).

- **Good judgement of people and situations**, and common sense in decision-making. The leader knows when to apply leadership behaviour conspicuously, for example, when to challenge or when to delegate. Experience counts, as well as time for thought and the modesty of consultation.

- **Ability to think on one's feet**, a combination of risk-taking, communication skills and honesty; admired by many, but can easily become 'shooting from the hip.'

Some of these attributes become evident as the leader acts out his various roles, while some are never given an opportunity to display themselves. However, the Eleven Roles and the other leadership attributes are always in evidence in times of change, and change cannot happen without leadership and the leader's acceptance of his roles.

> The role of the leader is a complex one, riddled with ambiguity, incompatibility and conflict. *(Charles B. Handy)*

What others have written

James M. Kouzes and **Barry Z. Posner**, in their book *Credibility*, refer to a research project in which 15 000 people were asked the question, *"What makes a good leader?"* The answers were given in broad descriptive terms:

- Fair-minded, co-operative, honest: 87%
- Imaginative/forward-looking: 71%
- Inspirational: 68%
- Competent: 58%

[Three of these criteria for good leadership cover several of the Eleven Roles listed in this book. 'Fair-minded, co-operative, honest' refers to Trust, Integrity and Delegation. 'Imaginative' comes under the heading of Vision and Challenge, and 'Inspirational' under Communication. But when we read 'Competent' as a criterion for good leadership, we question what is meant. Competent as a leader? As a manager? As a technician?]

Kouzes and Posner make the further point that leaders with high credibility foster such things as pride in the organisation, a spirit of co-operation and teamwork, and feelings of ownership and personal responsibility. They write that credible leaders

- do what they say they will do
- link their actions to the wishes of their supporters
- believe in the value of others
- can make a difference to the lives of others, including releasing the leader in others

- admit their mistakes
- arouse positive and optimistic feelings
- create a climate for learning and development.

[These are laudable and positive aspects of effective leadership, a list to be used by supporters (followers) when they are asked to pass judgement on leadership behaviour. Such judgement is likely to be black-and-white, with no shades or degrees of effectiveness.]

In their 'Leadership Practices Inventory' **Kouzes and Posner** write that Leadership is an observable, learnable set of five practices:
- Challenging the Process
- Inspiring a Shared Vision
- Enabling Others to Act
- Modelling the Way
- Encouraging the Heart

John Adair lists the essential qualities of leadership as initiative, perseverance, integrity, humour, tact, compassion, efficiency, industry, audacity, honesty, self-confidence, justice, moral courage and consistency.

John Kotter's list of personal attributes for leadership includes the need for industry and organisational knowledge, good relationships within the firm and the industry, reputation and track record, keen mind, good judgement, ability to think multi-dimensionally, empathy, ability to sell and persuade, integrity and motivation.

Jan Grant lists qualities in women that are especially relevant to leadership:
- communication and co-operation
- affiliation and attachment
- power (caring and nurturing)
- physicality (reality)
- emotionality, vulnerability and lack of self-confidence (expressing emotion, accurate self-assessment).

Judy Rosner noticed that women leaders differentiate themselves from men by their interactive style. They encourage power-sharing, participation and information exchange. Their actions enhance their followers' sense of self-worth, and energise them.

> Successful corporate leadership requires intellect and business acumen, of course, but also humility, self-awareness and generosity. *(Steve Newhall, MD, Development Dimensions International, Europe.*

Food for thought

Study of leadership characteristics raises the question: is leadership transferable? If a manager can transfer his allegiance, with his managerial skills, to another workplace, can a leader move equally easily from one environment to another? Are there influences on his success as a leader which cannot be replicated? How do 'followership' and environment interact with the leader's actions to generate success or the other thing? Come to that, how do we measure the performance of a leader? Against what criteria? Indeed, is a leader's performance to be measured at all? By whom?

Some – not all – of these questions are addressed elsewhere in this book.

> Leadership – is mystical. Then let us not pretend to understand it. *(Bombardone in "Geneva" by George Bernard Shaw).*

Leadership and Management

The roles of leadership and the function of management are distinct and complementary, and full of paradoxes. The effective manager adopts leadership behaviour when the situation calls for it, when change is a priority. The CEO adopts leadership behaviour all the time. Future leaders will be young, drive change and team up with experienced professional managers. Multi-cultural and 'virtual' work groups present extra challenges for the leader.

A United Technologies advertisement started, "People don't want to be managed, they want to be led. Whoever heard of a world manager? World leader, yes. Educational leader. Political leader. Scout leader. Business leader. They lead, they don't manage."

Business leader? Maybe this is a new concept for those managers who have been raised in the traditions of business and industry, where hierarchy and order flourish. According to John Farrow, "complex organisations staffed with motivated professionals" (a description of most national and multi-national businesses) "now need leaders first and managers second." And Morris, Willcocks and Knasel write, "…leadership is the all-important 'Ingredient X' that is missing from too many… organisations."

In many books on management theory and practice, the words 'Leader' and 'Leadership' are used interchangeably with 'Manager' and 'Management', so that the reader is left with the impression that they are one and the same. For example, John Adair suggests that the leader's job is to manage tension with a functional approach, by

- defining the task
- planning
- briefing
- controlling
- evaluating
- motivating
- organising
- setting an example.

Six of these functions (*motivating* and *setting an example* are the exceptions) are key components of the traditional managerial function. They not only permit little demonstration of leadership behaviour, but at times even discourage its application. But John Adair has recognised that some management skills are necessarily linked to leadership behaviour.

Let's look at what Charles B. Handy has to say about management: *"Management has become at least a semi-profession . . . a recognised occupational role."* True – and using the term 'profession' emphasises a distinction between management and leadership, the difference between the studied function of manager and the complementary role of leader. But they are not mutually exclusive: a manager becomes more effective and productive when he adopts leadership behaviour, while a leader needs to have and practise management skills. As we have read before, John P. Kotter writes, *"Leadership complements management: it doesn't replace it."* Leadership is one of the key tools of today's manager.

> Management is not about controlling people – not about liking people – it's about putting their strengths to work. *(Alfred P. Sloan)* [In other words, it's about adopting leadership behaviour in order to be effective as a manager.]

Here's a list of some of the characteristics of the manager's *function*, disregarding for the moment leadership behaviour:

Management

1. is a function, a job, a title assigned by others
2. is left-brain, a controller
3. is the analysis, sequencing, the time-bound specific application
4. is objective, precise, unemotional
5. is a task
6. is seeing what should be
7. uses a road map
8. is essential for stability
9. may be a burden to the owner
10. ordains
11. cannot be shared
12. in a group, is always vested in one person
13. is accepted by those who are managed

14. can be learned by experience

15. must be learned by precept and example

16. can be practised by oneself

And a **manager**:

17. focuses on the mission

18. maintains the status quo, plans orderly progress

19. takes care, is prudent

20. needs time to think and act

21. has a book of rules to guide him

22. is given power, may abuse it; is rewarded

23. is judged on his performance as manager

24. is often a prisoner of events

25. is concerned about his next assignment, doesn't think about his successor

26. does things right

27. gives orders, monitors performance

(The numbers do not indicate priorities: they are only for the purpose of making comparisons with the list of characteristics of leadership and leaders that follows.)

These are exactly the characteristics and actions that are sought in managers in ideal, unreal stable situations:

- where change is not expected
- where continuity and stability are required
- where harmony has been achieved.

They often form the basis of managers' job descriptions, performance appraisal and training.

Let's look at the characteristics of the leadership *role* compared with those listed above for management, and add them to the *function* of a manager-as-leader.

Leadership

1. is a role for anyone to adopt

2. is right-brain, high-powered

3. is an art, a philosophy

4. relies on emotion for communication, energy, drive

5. is behaviour and attitude

6. is seeing what could be

7. uses a compass

8. is essential for change

9. makes the owner feel good

10. enables, trusts and empowers

11. can be shared

12. in a group, can change from moment to moment

13. is respected by those who are led

14. can be developed in oneself and others

15. can be communicated by example

16. is evident only in the response of the followers

And a **Leader**

17. focuses on the vision

18. makes people uncomfortable about the status quo, tolerates chaos

19. takes risks, is courageous

20. knows when to make haste

21. asks questions, listens to the answers

22. accepts the responsibility of power

23. is judged on his performance as Leader

24. creates events, seizes opportunities

25. develops his successor

26. does the right things

27. delegates, trusts, empowers; leads by example

This second list is not a list of ideals, nor of ways to achieve perfect leadership. Some of these characteristics can dangerously result in the leader's isolation from the rest of his group. He could be perceived as a guru on a mountain-top, or as a general leading the troops from a room in the Ministry. Such an unproductive situation can be avoided if the leader is seen to share the 'blood and bullets' in the way that most managers in fact do.

And, comparing the second list with the first, it is obvious that there are paradoxes and contradictions. For instance, the leader is expected to use emotion when communicating, yet as a manager his behaviour is objective and precise. But this is normal, flexible behaviour. Emotion is a valid behavioural tool when communication is to be positive and inspiring, when for example the leader describes his vision to the group. But objectivity is more appropriate when, for example, a plan of action is under discussion. Another paradox (there are plenty in the two lists) is seen where the manager ordains, while the leader enables, trusts and empowers. The manager must sometimes adopt an unyielding attitude when giving orders, but he demonstrates his trust by delegating, and facilitates by smoothing the delegate's path and empowering him with appropriate authority.

An effective leader uses all the weapons at his command, choosing from his armoury according to the situation. Flexibility and adaptability are vital.

> There is a difference between leadership and management. Leadership is of the spirit, compounded of personality and vision; its practice is an art. Management is of the mind, a matter of accurate calculation... its practice is a science. Managers are necessary; leaders are essential. *(Field Marshal Lord Slim, quoted by John van Maurik)*

What others have written

Manfred Kets de Vries offers a list of comparisons between managers and leaders:

Manager	Leader
Present	Future
Stability	Change
Short term	Long term
Instruction	Inspiration/vision
Goals determined by immediate need	Goals based on "Inner Theatre"
How?	Why?
Position based on authority	Charisma
Control	Empowerment
Complexity	Simplicity
Logic	Intuition
Corporate concerns	Social/corporate concerns

[While this is a useful summary of the chief contrasts between managers and leaders, Kets de Vries omits several attributes of leadership that are essential for success.]

Kets de Vries also emphasises that effective leaders are good at building and maintaining communications networks, while **Judy Rosner** writes that women leaders attribute their power to networking (as well as to charisma and interpersonal skills). This networking theme is repeated by **Kouzes and Posner,** who point out that successful managers are seen to develop an effective web of relationships, and by **Howard Gardner**, whose exemplary leader broadens his large, heterogeneous circle of contacts. **Robert Kelley** highlights the need, in a knowledge economy, for personal and responsive networks, including the need for correct interpersonal skills and etiquette to use these networks to maximum advantage. Finally, on the subject of networking, **John Kotter** suggests that effective business leadership creates an agenda for change and builds a strong implementation network.

As far as business leadership is concerned, **Warren Bennis** describes it as having four basic ingredients: a guiding vision, passion, integrity, and curiosity and daring. **Douglas Ready** analysed the results of interviews in 1993 of nearly 1500 managers, and concluded *inter alia* that the five most important future capabilities of managers would be visioning, empowerment, leading change, providing results and customer focus. Future CEOs would have to meet the challenges of continually re-inventing the organisation's organisational capacity, broadening its leadership and knowledge capacity, and leveraging its mechanisms for regeneration and growth.

Charles B. Handy writes, *"The manager, like the [medical] general practitioner, is the first recipient of problems."* [True: perhaps some managers see their job as comprising only problems and interruptions. But the effective manager, while doing these things, also gives thought to the future of his work group, to the likely changes in the group's objectives and tasks, and the results that he believes the group should achieve. He whole-heartedly adopts leadership behaviour.]

According to **Victor Vroom,** there are three levels of management activity:

1. Strategic: the manager sets direction in response to a changing environment, and assigns resources.
2. Leadership: he puts in place cultures that will link the strategic direction with the operational level to enable the operational level to carry out its task.
3. Operational: he improves thinking and problem solving.

Under the heading of Leadership, Vroom offers us the opportunity of integrating the Eleven Roles into the manager's basic portfolio of activities, thus establishing and applying behaviours that ensure success of the group's endeavours. [But we must challenge his assertion that the manager can 'improve thinking' – reflecting either optimism in the manager's skills or a godlike talent.]

Douglas McGregor labels two managerial approaches as Theory X and Theory Y. The Theory X manager believes that people dislike work, will avoid it if possible, and need to be coerced, motivated ("incentivized"), directed and controlled. The Theory Y manager believes that, for the average human being, work is as natural as play. People direct themselves, commit themselves to satisfying their egos, seek responsibility. Creativity and intellectual potential are widely distributed and only partially used.

Companies today need leaders more than they need managers. *(John P. Kotter)*

Distinct and Complementary

This book is about leadership behaviour that is required of managers continuously and intensively, behaviour which is inherent and whose effectiveness can be developed. It is not about management skills that are acquired through training and experience. It also aims to explain the distinction between management and leadership, a distinction which is sometimes a conflict, but always complementary. Today's managers would do well to heed the words of a former CEO of DuPont in a speech to his senior managers:

Leadership is not professional development, although the two go hand in hand in the modern corporation. Professional development is the sort of thing that can be planned through courses, programs and work experience. Leadership, on the other hand, is a character trait. It may be a gift or it may

105

be cultivated, but it cannot be automatically instilled.

All genuine leaders have two things in common. First, they have the ability to enable people to confront reality in a way that they see opportunity and potential for success even when the immediate situation poses problems. And second, at some level, leaders make people feel constructively uncomfortable about the status quo. If you want change, you want leadership. If you are content with the status quo, you want a caretaker.

I have quoted Ed Woolard word for word, but if I had been making this speech, I would have used "manager" in place of "caretaker." (But Ed couldn't do that, could he, with about eight thousand managers in his organisation?) Later in the speech he says:

To do that [to achieve the vision he has described] we are going to need an attitude of leadership throughout our organisation. This is distinct from an attitude of management, and there's a reason for that. An attitude of management is most effective when the political and economic climate is generally predictable: when the organisation can make stepwise progress towards its goals; when the need to take risks in order to succeed is minimal; and when there is time. Nowhere in the world do those conditions hold today.

Throughout this book, we take Ed's words further, and see what today's – and tomorrow's – leaders need to be and to do. By defining leadership in terms of its Eleven Roles, and by showing where even the best managers may be under-estimating and under-using their leadership talents (and how they can do something about it), this book can raise awareness of leadership as a potent source of organisational energy, drive and motivation. As a result, it can help managers, present and future, to sharpen their leadership behaviour ready for the occasion when the priority is change, and leadership is called for.

> When Noah designed an ark and gathered his family and a pair of male and female animals of all species to survive the Great Flood, he demonstrated his natural leadership. But when he turned to his wife and said, "Make certain the elephants don't see what the rabbits are doing", he was being a far-sighted and practical manager, with skills based on hard experience. *(Ben Rich, "Skunk Works")*

A good manager may not be able to demonstrate his leadership qualities, either because he doesn't have to (when change is not a priority) or because he doesn't have the opportunity, because changes are insignificant or because other people take the leadership for the change process. But the potential is always there, waiting to be released in the right situation (Churchill led well in war, less well in peacetime). And the good manager knows that leadership behaviour adds value to his management skills; it is a key criterion for success as a manager. He is judged less on how he handles the 'mechanics' of his managerial duties and more on the ways in which he has inspired and enabled his group to achieve the results expected of it.

With his manager's hat on, the manager in reality has also has 'stuff to do' such as being a magnet for problems (absence, complaints, shortage of resources, etc.), fighting fires and handling small tasks. His time is fragmented, with one problem unsolved before another is presented. His work is composed of interruptions. With his leader's hat on, the same person demonstrates leadership behaviour – he dreams, he challenges, he delegates, and he does things right. He separates the important from the urgent, the big from the small. He values time as a finite, non-renewable resource. He acts as a bridge between the old and the new, between the outside and the inside, between people.

The change from manager to leader and back can be instantaneous, brief and endlessly repeatable. It requires energy and dedication, self-control and trust – and is highly satisfying and effective. To know that one has leadership talent in plenty, and knows how to use it effectively, is the most satisfying aspect of management that can be imagined.

> In her "African Laughter", a beautiful and wise account of four visits she made to Zimbabwe, Doris Lessing says she saw this poster on a wall of a government office in Harare:
>
> The Boss drives his men,
> The Leader inspires them.
> The Boss depends on authority,
> The Leader depends on goodwill.
> The Boss evokes fear,
> The Leader radiates love.
> The Boss says 'I',
> The Leader says 'We'.
> The Boss shows who is wrong,
> The Leader shows what is wrong.
> The Boss knows how it is done,
> The Leader knows how to do it.
> The Boss demands respect,
> The Leader commands respect.

So be a Leader,

Not a Boss. *(The Economist, November 1992.)*

[But there are times when bossiness is needed. It's a matter of judgement and flexibility in adopting the appropriate approach to the issue.]

Leading a multi-cultural group

Increasingly, groups comprise people from different backgrounds. In Britain, this can mean not only Scots, Welsh and Irish, but also people whose origins lie in India and Pakistan, or in the islands of the Caribbean or, more recently, in one or more of the other 26 member countries of the European Union. Leading a group with this kind of mixture calls for additional skills.

> Leadership is recognition that the unique and essential function of leadership is the manipulation of culture. *(Edgar H. Schein)*

First of all, the leader must be aware of possible communication difficulties. If the leader is an English-speaker (and, one has to ask, in which dialect?), he will need to tolerate slower understanding of his spoken and written messages. Slower, but not less complete. Group members are, we assume, no less intelligent and dedicated than he is himself, but where English is a person's second language, there is frequently a delay in grasping the fine detail of the message. And the leader may find it necessary to restrict the use of 'fancy' language, with which English abounds, and keep his messages simple (as Winston Churchill often suggested). A message, in all situations, needs to be given with a crushing desire for understanding. In the same way, the leader may need to be tolerant of others' lack of fluency in English, and make allowances for their inability to make themselves understood. Paraphrasing becomes second nature to everyone involved, to ensure understanding.

Then the leader needs to take account of the cultural differences of group members. In a multi-cultural group, not only are they different from him, but they may also be different from each other, which means that expectations and values – of organisation, of work-pattern, of relationships – differ from one person to another. The leader will need to follow the precepts given in the chapter on Followership (page 21), and aim to understand the needs of each individual in the group. Only by informing himself about each person can the leader hope to meet every need within the group.

It is impossible to generalise here about the kinds of cultural differences that a leader may have to contend with; but awareness of likely problems is enough to cause a leader to take extra care when dealing with a multi-cultural group.

If you want to lead the people, walk behind them. *(Lao Tzu)*

Leadership of 'virtual' teams

In many organisations, leaders are being asked to handle groups or teams of people who have no common 'home' or workplace. They are always knowledge workers, and may be spread out across a country, or over international boundaries. They may not even speak the same language – yet as a group they have a common goal and direction. These virtual teams not only present the sort of challenge that multi-cultural groups offer, but in addition are inter-connected only electronically – by telephone and e-mail – to the team's leader. There may be little or no face-to-face communication between team members, and between the group and its leader. How can the manager maintain his position in this situation?

Leadership behaviour is just as important in these situations as in conventional, office-based ones. Communication is the most important Role here, not only between the leader and team members but, just as important, also between the leader and the managers (bosses) to whom team members report, and with whom they work. Every team member has a dual allegiance, and it is a fact of life that his strongest ties are the 'tribal' ones to the people he works with. The leader must continually let those people know what is being asked of the team member *as a team member* and how this affects local work relationships. He must also ensure that team members respect each other's views and actions, and share each other's concerns.

The team leader can bring, and hold, the virtual team together by creating opportunities for collaboration on issues and problems that are common to all the team, and by ensuring that collaboration leads to practical results. For instance, if an IT team shares a common problem in introducing a new system into the organisation, it is good for the members of the team to share their views and their possible solutions to the problem – with the team eventually agreeing on the common solution that best meets the immediate need of each member of the team.

Not everyone qualifies as a member of a virtual team. Qualifications include an ability to communicate well (listening included), being a team player (which involves dedication to the team's goals and efforts), and acceptance that the team leader can only offer recognition, and rarely reward. Non-qualifiers are disruptive and, in the sensitive atmosphere of a virtual team, cannot be allowed to remain members.

Communications within a virtual team are mainly by telephone and e-mail, which exclude face-to-face conversation (which allows body language and facial expressions to be registered, as well as allowing 'natural' conversation, with more than one person speaking at a time). Phone calls must be well prepared, disciplined (no time for chat) and decisions confirmed in writing. Conference calls must be treated like meetings, with agendas and minutes to ensure the orderliness of the process. E-mails must be used carefully (sometimes a 24-hour space between writing and sending is advisable). In fact, *virtually* all the advice given in the chapter on Communications, and in the paragraph above on leading a multi-cultural team, applies, with special attention to the importance of clarity of message in both directions.

Sharpen your Leadership behaviour as a Manager

- Set the right example.
- Trust, delegate, empower.
- Make the decisions that are yours to make.
- Merit the trust of the people who report to you.
- Take time to think and plan strategically.
- Think more could-be, less should-be.
- Aim to understand the needs of each individual in the group.
- Improve your communication skills (speaking, writing, listening).
- Watch how leaders in voluntary organisations perform.
- Develop your successor.
- Ask "Why not?" and not "Why?"
- Take risks.
- Tolerate mistakes.

Leadership at the Top

There is no reason why the Eleven Roles of the Leader should not apply to those at the top of the corporate hierarchy – the Chairman, the Chief Executive Officer, the Managing Director, the Owner – who are all accountable to shareholders, employees, customers and suppliers for the success of the enterprise. The pressures are considerable, and leadership behaviour is essential for the success and survival not only of the individual but also of the business. Let's look at the CEO as an example of leadership – *strategic* leadership.

The Eleven Roles of the Leader constitute a major part of the working life of the CEO, who has relinquished most of his managerial duties (which included *organisational* leadership). The CEO questions every move that he himself makes, and constantly challenges those who report to him, in order to stimulate the highest quality of decision-making. Vision comes from the 'helicopter effect', from taking time to view the present situation objectively and to focus energy on the factors which will influence the business in the future. The mastery of change, involving continuous assessment of risk, is indispensable behaviour by an effective CEO. Skilful delegation is naturally a part of the CEO's stock-in-trade – without it, he would drown in paper and meetings.

People clamour for direction ("Tell me what to do.") And it is the Directors of a business who guide them. Not only are most CEOs consummate visionaries ('pilots'), masters of change ('transformers') and skilful delegators, but they are also highly effective communicators. They demonstrate out-of-the-ordinary skills of persuasion; they are shrewd listeners.

> I spend one tenth of my time deciding on strategy and the rest of my time communicating it. *(Percy Barnevik, when Chairman of Asea Brown Boveri).*

To continue with the list of leadership roles, a CEO without trust in his lieutenants rapidly finds himself isolated and abandoned; he needs their support and their experience. His integrity is taken for granted. A CEO, mature and experienced, knows himself well enough to exploit his strengths and make allowance for his weaknesses, and he encourages others to develop themselves, with an eye on his succession.

All these are leadership behaviours – the Eleven Roles. The rest of his many talents as CEO are management skills. So what raises a leader into the CEO function, apart from being in the right place at the right time and reflecting the image and management style of the 'selection committee'? It is most likely the demonstration of leadership behaviour consistently and with conviction that inspires the selectors to pick one person, out of many, to fill the CEO function and leadership role. In particular, the new CEO will have used his skills of persuasion to best effect, to speak up when appropriate, to cajole others into following his lead, to charm away resistance, to badger the recalcitrant and to publicly honour the enterprising.

But, when it comes to acting as a Hero in front of others, the CEO is not always perfection, for two reasons. First, he will probably have made greater effort to follow his chosen career path than to give loyalty to his corporate employer. Second and conversely, his dedication to his employer's business may be stronger than his allegiance to the people who work for him. For example, he may deal with legislators and competitors in aggressive, even offensive, ways which he would not wish others to copy. His behaviour may be influenced by his own role models – his predecessor, his idols, the CEO of a rival business. But if he accepts his responsibility as role model, he is open and assertive about his behaviour and is prepared to stand by it.

In future, the importance of role modelling will override many other leadership qualities. The CEO increasingly represents the company to shareholders, to investors, to customers, to suppliers and to the community, and takes responsibility for the conflicting demands of long-term and short-term results, and the demands of all these stakeholders.

What others have written

Jim Collins wrote (in the *Harvard Business Review*) that the common characteristics of the CEOs of eleven successful US companies included "a paradoxical mixture of personal humility and professional will." [Nothing paradoxical about it: their behaviour changed according to the situation. They demonstrated humility when adopting democratic behaviour, when they needed (because of uncertainty) to consult and to share decision-making. Their "professional will" became apparent when they assertively pushed through decisions and plans that could meet resistance. Effective leaders adapt their behaviour to the situation, naturally and without effort.]

Sir John Harvey-Jones writes that the art of being a top leader is one of breadth of understanding, absolute clarity of aims and lightness of actual intervention. Courage and risk-taking are essential, as well as careful selection of the followers (the board) whose task is to challenge the CEO.

The Future of Leadership in Management

As the technology-based world changes, so demography changes. The upsurge of youth at the helm, as entrepreneurs, masters of the new technologies and drivers of change, is resulting in a new form of business leadership, significantly different from yesterday's. This new style of leadership emphasises, and relies on, the difference between the manager's function and the leader's role.

> Because leaders and managers are basically different, the conditions favourable to one may be inimical to the growth of the other. *(Abraham Zaleznik)*

The first steps in this direction are already evident in the new way in which managers are being selected. Less emphasis is laid on skills acquired through training and experience, and more attention is being paid to the character and behaviour of the candidate. Today's selection process aims to establish

- how the candidate interacts with others
- how he views relevant issues
- his reaction to real or imagined events and situations
- his personal aspirations
- his dreams of the future of the business

– in short, how he would perform as a leader. Knowledge and skill are not ignored, but they are less important than before, and, in the case of 'knowledge workers', less easy to assess. Their knowledge will in any case be out-dated within a few years. Soft 'people' skills are seen as the key to effective management.

In the next steps towards the new ways of running businesses, leadership and management are being separated. Future *leaders* will be young and will wield, for a short time at least, sapiential authority to a high degree, leaving the *management* of the business to the older people, whose sapiential authority has declined with the changes in technology, but whose moral authority and maturity will counterbalance the energy and risk-taking of the youngsters. The experienced professional manager will emerge as a new class of employee, with skills devoted almost exclusively to managing people. He will hire and fire, allocate resources, and cherish and nurture the people in his care, who themselves will do the work that has outpaced him, under the leadership of young taskmasters.

On his side, the young leader will show that he has the talents needed to lead his businesses to success:

- he will have a vision, a barely achievable goal, that drives him and, in turn, the group he leads
- he will challenge every paradigm and question every assumption
- change and risk will be second nature to his energy and drive
- he will communicate well, albeit in the vernacular of his age and his technology
- he will trust others, and he will be trustworthy within the limits of his questioning attitude
- as an integral part of a productive, efficient group he won't need to delegate much – fortunately, because he won't do it well, having been raised in an age in which individualism is valued above esprit de corps

113

- he won't get involved in developing others, but he will have a thirst for knowledge and self-improvement that his energy will help him to satisfy
- and he'll be assertive, emotional, a self-starter, and a glutton for bench-marking against the competition.

As business learns to appreciate the merits of separating dynamic leadership from experienced management (we already see it in some sports and in some high-tech businesses), others will be influenced by its positive results to try it. We'll see it in industry, in voluntary organisations and, one day, in professions like accountancy and law. The professional 'people-manager' (the supervisor? the gaffer?) will be a new recognised function.

This change will bring innovation in the workplace. It will include

- selection processes in which emphasis is laid on a candidate's leadership qualities
- a carefully monitored probationary period during which a newly-appointed leader is tried and tested
- reverse coaching, in which the young teach the old how to handle the new technologies
- formal "third-career" learning programmes for mature people, who have plateaued in their 40s and need to develop new skills, even a non-competitive outside interest.
- even more early (or earlier) retirement
- development programmes to help young leaders adapt to their new role as manager as they burn out approaching "middle age".

Although the way in which the leader operates is changing, leadership behaviour will remain much the same. There will probably be a change of emphasis: vision, challenge and risk will become more widely encouraged, while the 'relationship' behaviours such as trust and coaching will be less used. People will increasingly take charge of their own development, and expediency will lessen the need for trust, delegation and trustworthiness.

> The Future is an opportunity to do new things rather than a trial to be endured. *(Anon)*

Decision-making and Problem-solving

Styles of leadership are strongly represented in the application of Creative Problem Solving tools to strategic and day-to-day issues.

> Be willing to make decisions. That's the most important quality in a leader. Don't fall victim to (what I call) the "Ready-aim-aim-aim-aim" syndrome. You must be willing to fire. *(T. Boone Pickens)*

Leadership style shows up clearly in the decision-making process. The leader has to determine, from one situation to another, the style he wants to adopt for this process. He may decide on the assertive style when time is short *and* he has self-confidence *and* he has information *and* he understands the degree of risk. His decision also takes into account "stakeholder symmetry" (a term coined by Warren Bennis) in which the claims of all who have a stake in the result are balanced. But if one or more of these criteria cannot be applied, he may prefer the co-operative style to allow for consultation and study, for the acquisition of data, and for sharing of uncertainty and risk. Creative Problem Solving (CPS) offers the leader a number of tools for the co-operative, the assertive or the conventional decision-making process.

> Successful leaders make decisions about situational and people interventions based not on their personal preferences but on what is called for by the situation. They are able to separate personal needs from the organisation's, or are able to manipulate the situation so that it better lines up with their preferences. *(Steve Zeisler).*

Leadership and Creativity

Today's business climate, and the climate in other spheres of human activity such as politics and voluntary work, demand creativity. Entrepreneurs are in great demand, and innovators are in short supply. *"There is no shortage of venture capital or of bright ideas, but there is a serious shortage of people with the ability to execute the ideas"* (The Economist, March 2000). Creativity is the war-cry of established businesses which hope to keep up in a rapidly changing world.

Just as everyone can lead in his own way, so each individual is creative in his own way. Creativity is not intelligence, personality or education. It's normal human behaviour, whose skills and discipline can be developed by everyone. It's often not original; it may involve plagiarism and imitation. It's invention, imagination, combination and connection. It's 'thinking outside the box'. It's inspirational – it generates satisfaction when successful. There is no individual whose creativity cannot be focused and tapped. And creativity means leadership. What is the link?

The best definition of leadership that I know is "Taking people where they haven't been before." Taking this thought a stage further, creativity may be defined as "The ability to use skill, experience and knowledge to create something of value that didn't exist before." The common factors are innovation and transformation, with energy as a catalyst.

> It's easier to change direction when you're moving than when you're stationary. *(Anon)*

Leadership exists only in times of change; in fact, change cannot take place without leadership. And creativity stems from a desire for change – discontent with the status quo and with "the way we do it around here" – and from the pain of deprivation and frustration. It's about innovation, providing solutions, meeting challenges. How can the power of creativity be harnessed to drive change? One way is through Creative Problem Solving (CPS), which relies on group performance to generate better answers.

CPS provides a number of tools for decision-making and problem-solving, which are precursors to the transformation process, and the discipline needed to maintain the momentum of the process. The three-stage CPS process relies on the group being led by the 'facilitator', a person who uses a range of skills and methods to bring out the best in the people forming the group. The facilitator may be the group's leader, or he may delegate the task to someone who can run the CPS process, with the leader joining in either as a group member, or as an observer (and critic, and source of information). In the absence of any kind of leadership, the group falls apart and the process comes to a standstill, and so leadership, or facilitation, is an integral component of the CPS process, and of the creativity involved.

Creative questions come before creative answers. Creativity is valueless if it's used in the wrong context: that's why, in CPS, so much energy and friction are generated in the first stage, "Understanding the Problem." And why so much importance is attached to being sure that the right problem is being solved. The leader encourages friction between group members to release creative energy. However, a perceptive touch is required to exploit the opportunities it creates.

CPS is a robust, wholly participative process for group involvement in solving problems, exploiting opportunities and creating a 'path forward'. It has been used for more than fifty years by businesses, educators, the military and other dynamic organisations to establish action plans, to meet the challenges of change, to initiate programmes for growth or survival and for countless other beneficial purposes. CPS is easy to apply: it simply requires a certain discipline to be fully effective. The process is a stimulating one, even fun at times, and participants emerge from a session inspired and keen to engage in the resulting plan. CPS is supported by a wealth of experience, in many countries and cultures, centred on its origins at Buffalo State University (www.cpsb.com).

Entry into the CPS process may be made at any of the three stages, and the way in which the group's leader (facilitator) uses the process demonstrates the style which he has chosen for the situation. His style may, of course, change from one problem to another; there is no reason to adopt the same style for every issue to be processed by CPS. The process is so vigorous that the group's leader may even absent himself from it – provided that he has briefed the group on the situation, given it all the data, and encouraged the group to appoint a facilitator (or named one himself).

Styles and the Three Stages of Creative Problem Solving

If the leader invites the group to enter the process at the first stage, "Understanding the Problem", his style can be labelled co-operative. The group is presented with a general statement of the situation, and invited to agree on the problem to be solved. This is often the most arduous, time-consuming and contentious of the three stages of CPS.

If, however, the leader defines the problem himself and starts the process at the second stage, "Generating Solutions", then his style is that of a conventional, middle-of-the-road, flexible leader who favours neither one extreme of style nor the other. He outlines the problem (as he sees it) to the group, invites it to identify all the possible solutions, and then to agree on the solution(s) which best suit the situation. He recognises that any solution arrived at in the group's deliberations may change with time:

- as new data arrive
- as the solution begins to bite
- as the people change

- as the problem itself changes.

Finally, if his group is confronted with not only a well-defined problem but also a solution, and is invited only to "Prepare an Action Plan" (the third and final stage of CPS), then the leader's style can be labelled assertive. He is, in effect, presenting a project to the group, which is then invited to fill in the organisational details, and thus to commit to it.

Sharpen your Decision-Making behaviour

- If it can be decided fast, do it. Decisiveness breeds respect.
- Use all the data, and study all the angles and options.
- Try to make the decision yourself. Write the pros and cons on paper.
- Prepare "what-ifs."
- If you involve others, listen carefully and expect to act on their advice (or to explain why not).
- Use Creative Problem Solving tools. Determine your approach and your style appropriate to the situation.
- Always keep the central or most important aspect of the current problem in mind.
- Know how to balance the chances on both sides of the decision, and keep these factors in proportion.
- Remain open to changing your mind in the presence of new facts.
- Avoid looking too far ahead, avoid looking for perfection and avoid making decisions that would be better postponed or not made at all.

Leadership in the Family

Parents and teachers are leaders of the young. They may not recognise nor realise their leadership potential.

> Every head of household should strive to be cheerful, and should never fail to show a deep interest in all that appertains to the well-being of those who claim the protection of her roof. *(Mrs. Isabella Beeton)*

Leadership behaviour is prominently displayed at home. In families, leadership is an obvious attribute for the heads of the household to display when dealing with domestic matters. Indeed, Stephen Covey, in "The 7 Habits of Highly Effective Families," writes that families mainly need leadership. As both parents go out to work and family life becomes ever more complex, *"The natural tendency of people is to provide more management."* But *"A well-led family does not require much management."* This highlights a significant difference between leadership and management at home.

At home, management can become a remote, non-contact process, while leadership requires face-to-face interaction. Use of management skills alone (look at the list on page 99) at home can lead to lack of contact in the family and its disintegration. Leadership behaviour, on the other hand, stimulates personal development, encourages exchange of ideas, and promotes trust and trustworthiness.

Parents as leaders

Children are ideal followers, hungry for guidance and direction, so they are ready and willing to be led into new experiences and relationships. After all, if leadership is defined as taking people where they haven't been before, children are the ideal people to take!

The Eleven Roles of the Leader easily fit into the pattern of parent/child relationship. The Coach is the most obvious; if parents show less than total concern for the development of their children, no amount of other leadership behaviour will compensate. On the negative side, there is evidence that where parents abdicate this role to the day-care centre, to school, to television and to computer games, their children show signs of frustration and rebellion. Coaching also covers development of the 'followers' as successors and, while most parents don't spend a lot of time thinking about succession and inheritance, it's an understood if unspoken part of family life.

The Role of The Rock, from father throwing his son into the air and catching him, to mother's words of wisdom to her daughter on her wedding day, are part of normal family behaviour. Communication skills, especially between the generations, are indispensable at all family levels. The role of Pilot isn't always evident, but there are few families in which some thought is not given to schooling, to holidays, to finances and to other strategic aspects of family life that impact on the children. Delegation of tasks, from car-washing to shopping, is another parental role in bringing up children. Upwards delegation, too, is normal – "Dad, will you walk the dog for me tonight (please)?"

Most parents adopt leadership behaviour automatically. However, parents who study the ways in which they relate to their children, and put effort into developing and adopting those particular leadership behaviours that are essential for the success of this relationship, find that family life is more rewarding and productive.

What can parents do?

Let's start with Communication. Talking and listening to your children are widely regarded as the keys to raising children well. Dinner-table conversation, father-son and mother-daughter chats (and cross-gender chats too!), and discussion of family issues as they arise, are important in a child's development. Encouraging children to express themselves (not only at school) will benefit every future adult, but only if he or she is taken seriously and answered in the same vein. "What do you think?" is a question that is rarely asked of, say, eight-year-olds, but it can elicit response, and generate ideas, that can astonish parents with their maturity and insight. But parents must have the patience to wait for the answer, even to flush it out with more questions, and take account of it in their deliberations.

The parents' vision of the future can and should be shared with the children, if they impact on the children's own lives. In fact, children often make significant contributions to the development of strategic plans, with their uncluttered view of what is possible. Children have fewer inhibitions, fewer negative experiences and less reason to fear the future than adults. They generate ideas that kindle innovative and creative solutions to family problems. And acceptance of these ideas creates confidence and self-sufficiency in the child.

Challenge is an important contributor to children's intellectual development. Parents and teachers can stimulate thought and energy by questioning (like a Coach) a child's ideas and notions and, in the event of apparent confusion, helping with explanation. Indeed challenge, in both directions, is a significant part of the teaching process.

Delegation and empowerment demonstrate trust, essential for a child's growth to adulthood. They encourage self-confidence, they engender trustworthiness, they provide opportunities for learning, and they foster independent action. Role-modelling, too, is an inescapable aspect of parenting (and of teaching). Children look up to parents and teachers as heroes, as mentors and guides, as sources of inspiration. This adulation may be tempered with the natural challenge and scepticism of the young, but the burden of responsibility lies on adults not to subvert children's ideals, but rather to set standards for children to follow.

Sharpen your leadership behaviour as a Parent

- Talk and listen to your children with interest, sincerity and care.
- Encourage children to express themselves. Take them seriously and respond in the same vein.
- Share your visions with the children, if they impact on the children's lives.
- Delegate tasks to children. Demonstrate trust.
- Challenge children's ideas. Invite a child to explain and justify his or her notions.
- Be aware of outside influences. Learn what is motivating and inspiring the child.
- Be honest and trustworthy in your dealings with children.
- Accept your role as Hero. Set an example for your children.

Leadership at School

Education offers many opportunities for leadership, in the classroom, on the field and in the staffroom and the principal's (head teacher's) office. Teachers behave as leaders. They complement the parents' role, with challenge, guidance, communication, trustworthiness, empowerment and other leadership Roles. They are heroes for their charges, in competition with children's peers and with their heroes in entertainment culture. Teachers are, of course, deeply concerned with their development.

The principal must add to these qualities trust, trustworthiness and 'people' skills such as personal development, since he has managerial responsibilities for the teaching staff. He does this in the face of the manager's dilemma, dealing with strategic issues at the same time as day-to-day problems. Principals find that delegation can be a useful tool, though it is hard for some former teachers to adopt this tool to ease their problems.

Children develop their own leadership behaviour. In school and elsewhere, increasing interaction with peers, as the child develops social attitudes, results in groups, gangs and clubs. In this way, the child is offered opportunities for leadership (for good or ill), and is aware of the responsibilities of role-modelling for the first time – also for good or ill.

Are they really leaders?

People in politics, in entertainment and in the military as well as business entrepreneurs are quoted as examples of leadership. Are they our Heroes? Are they role models for managers? And 'bad' leaders are a curse on society.

We have religious leaders, team leaders, discussion leaders, opinion leaders. They have their followers, who learn and take confidence from their leaders. Then there are people who claim the leadership role, or are deemed leaders as a result of being thus designated by the media and by popular acclaim. Who follows these people? Is their claim to leadership justified? Are they role models for an aspiring leader? Let's look at some of them.

Leadership in Politics

Many politicians exhibit certain essential leadership characteristics such as vision, challenge, persuasive communication, good judgement of people, drive and the acceptance of responsibility (not of leadership, but of service). But their vision may be tempered with short-termism and vote-catching populism. Their challenge, of each other, may be for parliamentary show rather than out of conviction. In other leadership criteria, politicians get poor grades. They are often branded as untrustworthy by the media and therefore by the electorate, they are seen to avoid risk, and they are not always models of high principle and rectitude; some are perceived as abusing the considerable privileges of their position.

Where political stability is the norm, major change is not part of the government's agenda. "[The function of government is] to confront crises and misfortunes, to deal with problems," said Lionel Jospin, the French prime minister in April 2001. These are situations in which leadership behaviour is valuable but not essential. Leadership is not a vital role in governments whose main tasks are to apply corrective action when things go wrong, and to tinker with the economy and the law, rather than to drive change. Politicians qualify as caretaker-managers and as professional administrators rather than as leaders. Apart from some leadership attributes, politicians are not good role models for managers in business and industry.

Voters don't always know what they want until politicians tell them.
That's called leadership, *(The Economist, October 2004)*

Leadership in Entertainment

Pop stars, sportsmen and other entertainers are in the public eye, and are therefore prime leadership material. However, many of them fail to realise their potential as leaders and role models for three main reasons:

1. they are isolated from the 'real world' by nature of their professions
2. they are rarely role models outside their professional activities
3. some are poor communicators.

Their asset is their technical skill which is neither a substitute nor a requirement for leadership. Emotion is the chief factor in the relationship between these modern heroes and their followers. Basking in reflected glory (celebrating, for example, the national team's win) or adulating a star on stage does little more than provide the followership with an outlet for emotional energy.

One can regret the lost opportunities for leadership among today's heroes. There are shining exceptions, however, and we can be grateful for the lead given by some popular figures who exploit their cult status in setting moral standards, in the fight against drugs and violence, and in relieving the afflictions of the destitute. These are the actions of effective leaders.

Leadership in the Military

> Leadership is the art of getting your subordinates to do the impossible.
> *(General George Patton)*

The armed forces are often quoted as examples of leadership in action. Indeed, whole books have been written on the subject, full of anecdotes and imagery of soldiers, from corporals to generals, demonstrating leadership behaviour. But the military is unsound as a source of leadership inspiration for leaders in business or in voluntary organisations. Because it is a fundamental necessity in time of war, a restricted form of leadership (and followership) is imbued in the military. Soldiers (and sailors, and airmen, and freedom fighters) are trained to obey commands without question, so that there will be no challenge to command or leadership when the moment for immediate action arrives. Unquestioning followership characterised by obedience is inculcated at all levels, necessary for survival in life-threatening situations. In the words of Admiral Lord Nelson, *"You must always implicitly obey orders, without attempting to form any opinion of your own respecting their propriety."* This attitude may have changed over two centuries, but not by much.

Leadership in these situations is therefore a matter of command and control, and few of the leadership roles that we have listed are useful or even acceptable. Take challenge: in the military; this is known as mutiny. Risk-taking, too, is discouraged; if it is practised at a staff level, 'cannon fodder' results. Delegation of authority is rare; levels of command and authority are precise. All in all, the military is not a suitable model of leadership for managers to emulate. But it's not all bad news: Colin Powell, ex-Chairman of the Joint Chiefs of Staff and latterly US Secretary of State, has said that in the military he had learned that *"Leadership is not rank, privileges, titles or money. It's responsibility."*

Entrepreneurs

Entrepreneurs have won a place in the affections of the media, for their drive and energy and, in some cases, extraordinary success. Some large businesses have even promoted 'intrapreneurship' in which managers are encouraged to copy the drive and risk-taking of successful entrepreneurs.

These businessmen are characterised as leaders because of their self-confidence and energy and their obsession with goals. An entrepreneur exhibits a number of leadership characteristics: he handles risk courageously, he obviously has conviction in his vision of the future, and he challenges and questions orthodoxy and others' ideas. And he may be perceived as charismatic – even superhuman. But, because he is obsessed with his enterprise, the entrepreneur may, just may, be arrogant, egocentric, insensitive and unable to delegate. He may be a poor communicator, and untrustworthy too. He may actively seek admiration and popular recognition.

Entrepreneurs may be idolised as 'leaders' by the media and vicariously by the man-in-the-street. They may well be perceived as role models for aspiring entrepreneurs, but they are not necessarily the best role models for aspiring leaders, because of their inadequacies in some leadership roles such as Mister Trustful and The Rock. However, the new breed of young, aggressive 'start-up' entrepreneurs, running dynamic high-technology businesses, can get away with their leadership failings through youthful drive and energy, and because they lead groups comprising ambitious people of their own inclination. (More about this in "The Future of Leadership in Management" on page 112).

Reason and judgement are the qualities of a leader. *(Tacitus, 55-130)*

What others have written

Manfred Kets de Vries suggests that some entrepreneurs start their own businesses because they have been difficult employees. They have low tolerance for subordinates who think for themselves. They have a need for recognition and applause. They see things in extremes when dealing with people, so their organisations lack a strong middle management: objective advice is sought from consultants.

'Bad' and ineffective leaders

There are 'good' leaders and 'bad' leaders. The judgement is that of the people and of history, using as criteria accepted principles of human behaviour, the emotional response to the leader's actions, and the outcome of the process of leadership. Good leaders abound, some of them self-effacing and unrecognised.

'Bad' leaders (an example is Adolf Hitler) have often caught public attention and devotion, and have thus caused or aggravated untoward situations on a large scale. What these people have in common, apart from a number of sound leadership characteristics, is one or more severely flawed traits. Lack of principle or of integrity, lack of vision, inability to communicate, inability to delegate – just one absent leadership trait may result in a 'bad' leader, however strong the other leadership characteristics may be.

A leader may not necessarily be a 'bad' leader, but an ineffective leader, because he

- doesn't listen
- doesn't delegate (or dumps what he dislikes doing)
- doesn't take risks
- communicates poorly
- doesn't trust anyone
- is untrustworthy
- doesn't help people to develop.

In addition to failing in one or more of the Eleven Roles of the Leader, an ineffective leader usually exhibits one or more of a number of further failings that render him unsuitable for the position. These failings include

- avoiding conflict (and aiming to be liked)
- fear of responsibility
- lack of vision and imagination
- tyranny
- self-centredness and selfishness
- seeking status and admiration
- arrogance
- abrasiveness and insensitivity
- indecision.

Ineffective leaders may also display a negative 'ivory tower' effect, in which they permanently separate themselves from their followers. Or they may see the organisation through rose-tinted spectacles, allowing complacency and optimism to replace drive and honesty.

Even a small degree of these weaknesses results in ineffective leadership. But take heart – an individual can correct or compensate for all of them, in order to improve his performance as a leader. Behaviour can be changed.

> Leadership appears to be the act of getting others to want to do something you are convinced should be done. *(Vance Packard)*

Myths and Misunderstandings of Leadership

Leadership has been misunderstood and idealised. Experience counts for more than training. A leader may misinterpret his role. Charisma could be a valid proposition.

Leadership has generated many myths and misconceptions, as sociologists and psychologists have tried to define and analyse it. Some of these myths, if believed, are damaging to the performance of the group or of individuals. For example, the notion that the leader has to be exceptionally skilled in the tasks of the group can undermine the confidence of other members of the group. It can also be an obstacle to the effective performance of the manager-as-leader, whose task is to inspire and co-ordinate the activities of the group rather than demonstrate competence in the individual skills that group members possess.

Leaders are not taller than others, nor older, nor more gifted in terms of scholastic aptitude. They are not smarter, or more intelligent, or better educated. They are not healthier, nor are only men capable of leadership; women are frequently more effective leaders than their male colleagues. Leaders are not necessarily 'good with people' (though communication skills are important, as are understanding and respect for people). Leaders are not necessarily the people elected to positions of power, nor those promoted into positions of authority. A leader does not need to be an authoritarian, nor does leadership require charisma to be effective.

> You don't have to be intellectually bright to be a leader. *(Sir Edmund Hillary)*. [And age and sex have nothing to do with it either.]

Trait theory, propounded by several writers, holds that leaders are in good health, or from upper socio-economic groups, or taller or shorter than average. While this may be true of some much-admired public figures, there are sufficient exceptions among the rest of the population to disprove this generalisation. Everyone has leadership potential, and no broad definition of a leader's personality and physique can be used to identify, or deny, potential for leadership.

> ...the enduring idea that leaders are somehow born and not made, that genetic make-up counts for more than training and experience. *(The Economist, March 2001)*. [We know that everyone has leadership potential. Experience, not training, makes an effective leader.] The

Economist article goes on: "Undoubtedly, some of the skills of leadership can only be learnt on the job. Today's empowered junior managers are better prepared to become leaders than were their predecessors."

Leaders are not trained, in the way that most managers are. The myth that leaders can be trained in leadership 'skills', assuming that they do not already possess them, can result in training programmes that fail because presumptive leaders are not receptive to being taught what they already know instinctively: also because participants may subsequently have little or no opportunity to practise their leadership behaviour. Leadership is inherent in everyone, and can be cultivated, developed and practised when opportunities are presented or created.

A leader doesn't need power to lead, and he needs but little authority (see pages 17 and 18) – though a manager needs lots of both to manage. Threats of sanctions are not in the leader's workbox. An effective leader has many carrots, few sticks.

The role of the leader may include that of figurehead, representative or ambassador of the group to outsiders, but these activities are incidental, not pivotal. The leader may also be credited with other attributes, including enthusiasm, sociability, patience, courage, decisiveness, faith and virility, to name a few. But none of these virtues is essential for effective leadership.

Some people in leadership positions misunderstand their roles as communicators. They seem to believe that

- speaking loudly or forcefully is necessary for leadership to be effective
- the leader does not need to smile, or display pleasure or humour, even when things are going right
- the leader must use pompous language and be long-winded when communicating
- the leader doesn't need to say 'Please' or 'Thank you' or 'I'm sorry.'

These people don't realise that 'being nice' to others is a way of earning their credibility and leadership credentials. Rudeness counteracts their effectiveness as leaders.

Yet leaders are not necessarily 'nice' people. The leader may be obsessed with his vision (temporarily or permanently) and blind to other more important or urgent matters. He may, like many of us, be under pressure to deliver. He may have problems peculiar to himself. He may be over-confident or overbearing. But his 'core' leadership behaviours, which generate trust and integrity and vision, can still be in place and enable the group, with him as leader, to function satisfactorily.

Charisma – not entirely a myth

The same thing may be said of charisma as Supreme Court Justice Potter Stewart said of pornography: "*I can't define it, but I know it when I see it.*" But while you might know charisma when you see it, do others know it too? Do you share the same view of the 'charismatic' leader as other people with whom he interacts? One man's hero may be another man's scoundrel.

> Charisma is any quality which sets a person apart and causes him to be treated as endowed with exceptional powers or qualities. *(Max Weber)*

Charismatic leaders are known for their effect on people's attitudes and behaviour. Jack Welch, Pat Buchanan, Adolf Hitler, Winston Churchill, Billy Graham, my former boss, many politicians – all are known for their charisma, for the ways in which they have charmed people, for better or worse. They have done this by using their communication skills most persuasively. Their speeches and their writings use emotion (sparingly) and demonstrate energy, conviction, righteousness. Their pronouncements smack of doctrine. They inspire, stimulate, seduce. In short, their audiences, followers all, are captivated and carried away with their persuasive arguments, and become devotees, first of the man, then of the principles he preaches.

What else do charismatic leaders have that other people don't? In general, there are some attributes that are common to these paragons:

- overt self-confidence
- forceful energy and drive
- enthusiasm, passion
- infectious optimism and courage
- intolerance of negative attitudes.

In general, charisma can be defined as the authority of personality. There may be more attributes – but would these leaders be charismatic without spell-binding communication?

People clamour for leadership ("Tell me what to do"). They admire a charismatic leader, and will follow a leader whom they esteem to the ends of the earth. Sometimes such leadership takes the wrong turning, and the whole group, like children following the Pied Piper, follows the demon-leader into chaos. But on the whole, charismatic leaders are a force for good, and their strongest leadership characteristic, persuasive communication, is to be encouraged and emulated. Added to the leader's charm and warmth, it helps people to feel good and to give of their best.

Some charismatic leaders walk a tightrope between credibility and mistrust. They display, for example, a commendably high degree of self-confidence, which some people view as arrogance and intolerance. Or a charismatic leader may take risks that his followers consider foolish, but if he gets away with them, his charisma is enhanced. Another charismatic leader may have visions that his followers cannot at first believe in, but if he helps them to accomplish these dreams, his charisma is undiminished.

Charisma can exist without some essential leadership characteristics, resulting in an incomplete and therefore flawed leader. For example, a leader may find it impossible to delegate, because of his lack of trust in group members, which springs from exaggerated self-confidence and a consequent over-estimation of his own competence. A charismatic leader may have problems in helping others to develop their personal skills, because he sees them as possible contenders for his position. (Entrepreneurs, as we have seen, exhibit some of these shortfalls.) But, in spite of these failings in his behaviour, he still enjoys the reputation of charisma because his leadership behaviour is well developed and effectively used. Even the softly spoken, quiet leader, like the practitioner of Zen Buddhism, can carry the 'charisma' label, because his speech is persuasive and full of value to the listener. The greatest orators know when to whisper for effect.

When someone is to be selected to fill a leadership position, charisma should be the last item on the list of requirements. A manager who is expected also to be a leader should be vetted for

- creativity in his forward thinking
- a healthy questioning attitude
- his communication skills
- his integrity
- his concern for others.

He should be able to demonstrate his willingness to share the 'blood and bullets' of the front line, as well as an ability to objectively evaluate the situation and plan appropriate action. All these criteria for selection may add up to charisma, but the selectors have no way of knowing for sure until the candidate has been given a chance to earn this credential from his followers.

Charisma is not a reliable basis for a programme to develop effective leadership. It cannot be labelled as a leadership characteristic, because of its existence solely in the minds of the followers, and therefore its volatility. A leader cannot claim or aspire to be charismatic – it is for the followership to say.

It is frequently a misfortune to have very brilliant men in charge of affairs; they expect too much of ordinary men. *(Thucydides, 471-401 BC)*

What others have written

John Adair writes that charisma is a much exploited notion when looked at solely in the modern context in which it is characterised as a mixture of good looks and public attractiveness. It is like a gloss of fresh paint which soon reveals a lasting inadequacy beneath. But he adds that the charismatic phenomenon is a special kind of gift whereby the followers endow the leader with some superhuman characteristics.

People who have helped me

I am indebted to several friends, helpers and community leaders in the preparation of this book. Some of them gave me ideas and references, while some inspired me without knowing it.

- Victor Flintham of Granville Sansom, who has fed me with ideas, sources and the fruits of his experience.

- Steve Zeisler of Zeisler Associates, who has inspired me to put my ideas into writing, and has given me ideas and encouragement.

- Tack Training International, whose "Leadership and Management" development programme in 1986 was one of the catalysts for this book.

- Andy Roxburgh, at the time Technical Director of U.E.F.A., whose keynote address to the S.G.I.S. Youth Conference at the International School of Geneva in 1996 really got me going.

- The Organisational Effectiveness team in DuPont, Geneva, in the 1980s, where I learned the value of the leadership role in a multi-cultural, multi-business organisation, and its relationship to the management function.

- Ed Woolard, CEO of DuPont in the 1980s, who demonstrated superlative leadership behaviour at the top of a multi-national company in the throes of change.

- Sarah Krasker, whose degree in psychology and training skills and experience have been of inestimable value.

- Judy McDermott-Krasker, who gave me many very useful suggestions at various stages in the preparation of this book.

- My wife Linda, whose leadership qualities at home, at work and in her leisure activities were exemplary.

- David McDermott, who gave me some useful tips on virtual teams and other aspects of leadership in a business setting

- John McDermott, whose put his valuable managerial experience at my disposal.

- Lars Gellerstad in Geneva, who read one of the drafts of this book and made very useful comments.

This is what I've read and heard

Some of the assertions in this book represent my personal views of leaders and leadership. These views are based on my own observation and on situations in which I have led, or been led by successful or 'lame-duck' leaders. Other views in this book are those of published writers who have studied leadership from their own personal perspectives or as part of funded research projects. Most of these authorities are listed in the bibliography which follows.

I have read many texts, and listened to any number of views, on leadership. I have also studied the details of four expensive 'leadership development' programmes. Some books, articles, prospectuses and speeches have added to my own ideas, and some have irritated me, in the way that they have used "leadership" as an alternative term for "management".

So the following list is personal and short, and definitely not comprehensive. For example, few of the many books on management themes are included, because that's not the subject of this book, and because few writers on management treat leadership as a separate subject. Similarly, I haven't included some of the books whose views on leadership are (in my opinion) irrelevant or inconsequential.

This list is of sources that I have studied and, in some cases, quoted, with respect for their scholarship, and delight that (in most cases) their views agree with mine.

- John Adair, "Effective Leadership"
- John Adair, "Leadership Skills" (CIPD 'Management Shapers' series)
- "John Adair's 98 Greatest Ideas for Effective Leadership and Management" (ed: Neil Thomas)
- Joseph Boyett and Jimmie Boyett, "The Guru Guide"
- William C. Byham, "Zapp"
- Marlene Caroselli, "Leadership Skills for Managers"
- William A. Cohen, "The Art of the Leader"
- Stephen R. Covey, "Principle-Centred Leadership"
- W. Edwards Deming, "Out of the Crisis"
- Gareth Edwards, Paul K. Winter and Jan Bailey, "Leadership in Management" (The Leadership Trust)
- John Farrow, "Getting Rid of Management" (Engineering Dimensions, October 1989)
- Roger Gill of the Leadership Trust, "Essays on Leadership"

- Daniel Goleman, "Emotional Intelligence"
- Daniel Goleman, "What Makes a Leader?" (Harvard Business Review, January 2004)
- Rudolf Giuliani, "Leadership"
- Charles B. Handy, "Understanding Organizations"
- Harvard Business Review, "Effective Communication"
- Sir John Harvey-Jones, "Making it Happen"
- Stephen J. Hayward, "Churchill on Leadership"
- Robert Heller, "Effective Leadership"
- David J. Hickson, C. R. Hinings, Derek J. Pugh, "Writers on Organizations"
- IMD Newsletter No.1, 1980, "Perspectives for Managers"
- Rosbeth Moss Kanter, "When Giants Learn to Dance"
- Manfred Kets de Vries, "The Challenge of Leadership" (Conference of the Institute of Personnel Development, 1986)
- John P. Kotter, "What Leaders Really Do" (Harvard Business Review, May/June 1980) and "Leading Change"
- Michael Maccoby, "Why People follow the Leader" (Harvard Business Review, September 2004)
- Joan Magretta, "What Management Is"
- Lorraine Monroe's presentation at the 1987 Conference of the Swiss Group of International Schools
- Margot Morrell and Stephanie Capparelli, "Shackleton's Way"
- Steve Morris, Graham Willcocks, Eddy Knasel, "How to Lead a Winning Team"
- Dr Kent Peterson, "The Leadership Paradox"
- Andy Roxburgh's address to students in Geneva in 1986
- Edgar H. Schein, "Organizational Culture and Leadership"
- Alfred P. Sloan, "My Years with General Motors"
- John Van Maurik, "Writers on Leadership" (summaries of the writings of Jeff Adair, Warren Bennis, John Kotter, John Harvey-Jones and many others)

Index

www.ingramcontent.com/pod-product-compliance
Lightning Source LLC
Chambersburg PA
CBHW032017170526
45157CB00002B/736